T0090742

Cambridge Elements ≡

Elements in Publishing and Book Culture
edited by
Samantha Rayner
University College London
Leah Tether
University of Bristol

READING SPACES IN MODERN JAPAN

The Evolution of Sites and Practices of Reading

Andrew T. Kamei-Dyche
Aoyama Gakuin University

CAMBRIDGE
UNIVERSITY PRESS

Shaftesbury Road, Cambridge CB2 8EA, United Kingdom

One Liberty Plaza, 20th Floor, New York, NY 10006, USA

477 Williamstown Road, Port Melbourne, VIC 3207, Australia

314–321, 3rd Floor, Plot 3, Splendor Forum, Jasola District Centre,
New Delhi – 110025, India

103 Penang Road, #05–06/07, Visioncrest Commercial, Singapore 238467

Cambridge University Press is part of Cambridge University Press & Assessment,
a department of the University of Cambridge.

We share the University's mission to contribute to society through the pursuit of
education, learning and research at the highest international levels of excellence.

www.cambridge.org
Information on this title: www.cambridge.org/9781009181037

DOI: 10.1017/9781009181020

First published 2023

A catalogue record for this publication is available from the British Library.

ISBN 978-1-009-18103-7 Paperback
ISSN 2514-8524 (online)
ISSN 2514-8516 (print)

Reading Spaces in Modern Japan

The Evolution of Sites and Practices of Reading

Elements in Publishing and Book Culture

DOI: 10.1017/9781009181020

First published online: March 2023

Andrew T. Kamei-Dyche

Aoyama Gakuin University

Author for correspondence: Andrew T. Kamei-Dyche, akameidyche@gmail.com

ABSTRACT: This study provides an accessible overview of the range of reading spaces in modern Japan, and the evolution thereof, from a historical perspective. After setting the scene in a short introduction, it examines the development of Kanda-Jinbōchō, the area of Tokyo that has remained for a century the location in Japan most bound up with books and print culture. It then considers the transformation of public reading spaces, explaining how socioeconomic factors and changing notions of space informed reading practices from the early modern era to the present. This led, in turn, to changes in bookstores, libraries, and other venues. Finally, it briefly considers the nature and impact of virtual reading spaces, such as the representation of reading and reading spaces in popular culture and new modes of reading mediated by the digital realm, as well as the multifaceted relationship between these and older forms of reading practice.

KEYWORDS: reading, bookstores, libraries, book towns, Japan

ISBNs: 9781009181037 (PB), 9781009181020 (OC)

ISSNs: 2514-8524 (online), 2514-8516 (print)

Contents

1 Introduction

In recent years, reading has been a frequently covered topic in the Japanese mass media – specifically, concern over the practice of reading, or, rather, the apparently increasing lack thereof among youth. Cultural critics have bemoaned adults abandoning novels in favor of smartphone games and the arrival of a generation of children showing far less interest in leisure reading than did their parents and grandparents.[1] Reading spaces, particularly public ones – libraries, bookstores, cafes, and so forth – are increasingly invoked in a nostalgic manner, or in a fearful one, as if their decline is surely imminent amidst a willfully illiterate population. This discourse, however, usually lacks a historical element, instead deploying the trope of some hoary "traditional" past wherein everyone experienced reading in the same way from the early modern era until only recently.[2]

The reality is that over the course of the mid-nineteenth and twentieth centuries the wide-ranging socioeconomic transformation that Japan experienced led to changes in both the practice and the conception of reading. Increased access to education ushered in rising literacy that, coupled with

---

[1] Such articles tend to appear in response to surveys indicating declining reading habits among youth, such as the ones on student lifestyles produced by the National Federation of University Co-operative Associations (NFUCA) (the most recent being the fifty-sixth, based on data from October and November 2020; see NFUCA, 2021). Criticism is not limited to the print mass media: typical articles by online journalists and commentators include "Youth loss of interest in books is serious: More than half of university students read nothing daily" (Tomozō, 2018), or "Youth who don't read books: Is it because the Net is the best? Thinking about why we should read books" (Ichita, 2018). See the end of Chapter 3 and early Chapter 4, however, for another perspective on the surveys.

[2] What contemporary critics consider traditional Japanese reading – people quietly reading by themselves either for entertainment or, more ideally, to better themselves – is itself, however, largely a modern phenomenon, as we shall see. The collapse of the entirety of the Japanese reading experience into a single idealized category comes as no surprise to Japanese historians, who, like historians elsewhere in the world, have witnessed all manner of modern phenomena being read back into the past and reconceptualized as "tradition."

cheaper printing and the dramatic expansion of the book trade, ushered in an era in which by the dawn of the twentieth century being well-read was the mark of a sophisticated modern citizen. The elite associations of reading rapidly gave way as the century wore on, however, while reading practices also shifted: through the postwar years, patterns of social reading among family and friends declined and reading became an increasingly private endeavor. As reading changed, so too did reading spaces, which continually evolved in response. Contrary to the writers bemoaning the end of reading and reading spaces in Japan, both are still going strong – albeit, in many ways, in forms unthinkable a century ago. My goal in this work is to take you on a tour of reading in modern Japan, from modernization to postwar reconstruction and on to the digital age, by considering from a historical perspective just how and why reading practices changed and the impact this had on reading spaces.

1.1 Reading Spaces?

In the most straightforward conception, a reading space is simply a space associated with reading: it may be a space specifically designed for the activity of reading, or one in which reading occurs with a degree of regularity. Reading spaces could also include spaces for *readers*, such as locales in which to procure or discuss reading materials. Of course, these concepts frequently overlap: libraries and bookstores offer spaces in which to both acquire and read books, while spaces that primarily serve another purpose may also provide the opportunity for reading, and even furnish materials (I recall my student days spent reading through stacks of manga [comics] at noodle shops with friends).

Reading spaces therefore exist not only as sites connected to reading – whether in physical geographical or digital virtual space – but also as social spaces that connect readers through shared experience and identity as readers. When John Agnew defined place in terms of a "meaningful location," he identified three key characteristics: location, locale, and sense of place.[3] Regardless of whether its actual location is physical or virtual, a reading space would be one in which the locale (material arrangement or setting, as a context for activity) and sense of place (emotional and personal attachment, what it "feels like" to be somewhere) are fundamentally associated with reading

---

[3] Agnew (1987).

and/or readers. It is this admittedly loose, inclusive conception of reading spaces that I employ in the current work.

While Japanese literature has received significant scholarly and popular attention, including outside Japan, to say nothing of the enormous popular print culture phenomenon that is manga, the sites and practices of reading have received little attention. Though the current work will touch on many aspects of Japan's vibrant and evolving reading culture in modern times, its primary purpose is to sketch the spatial landscape in which this culture developed. While by no means exhaustive, it represents an attempt to outline some key aspects of the history of reading in modern Japan through its attendant spaces, and to prompt consideration of how reading and its social context influence each other. It is a story that is loosely organized both thematically and chronologically as it moves through three loci. Chapter 2 looks at the book town of Kanda-Jinbōchō, for more than a century the capital of Japan's print culture, and focuses on the late nineteenth and early twentieth centuries. Chapter 3 considers the transformation of public reading spaces, especially libraries and cafes, in light of broader socioeconomic and intellectual changes in Japanese society, and takes the story up through the postwar era to recent years. Finally, Chapter 4 turns to virtual reading spaces, touching on the representation of reading spaces in popular culture and the emergence of new modes of reading, and concentrates on the late twentieth century to the present.

Modern Japanese Historical Eras

Edo	江戸	1603-1868	*Early Modern Japan*
Meiji	明治	1868-1912	
Taishō	大正	1912-1926	
Shōwa	昭和	1926-1989	*Modern Japan*
Heisei	平成	1989-2019	
Reiwa	令和	2019-	

2 Kanda-Jinbōchō: Tokyo's Book Town

If we begin with the most obvious form of reading space, that of geographical or physical space, one space in Japan is more closely associated with reading than any other, but it is not a famous library, school, or publishing house – although it includes many prominent examples of all three. It is Kanda-Jinbōchō, Tokyo's book town, and nowhere else in the country is one likely to encounter so many people and institutions connected to and celebrating the act of reading.[4] While a major center for education and the publishing industry, it is most famous for its great number of used bookstores.[5] The town, in short, serves as a spatial representation of the production, retail, and consumption of books. This chapter will introduce the town and its history, which helps reveal how the Japanese reading world transformed within the context of modernization in the late nineteenth and early twentieth centuries.

2.1 A Stroll through Kanda-Jinbōchō

Western, and particularly European, readers may be more likely to think of picturesque villages when imagining book towns, given the association of the concept with a form of revival of rural communities begun in the 1960s and exemplified by the Welsh town of Hay-on-Wye. The scholar Jane Frank, for instance, relies on this definition – a conception shared by the International Organisation of Book Towns – and distinguishes book towns from what might be called cultural quarters in urban centers.[6] From this perspective, Kanda-Jinbōchō would clearly be an instance of the latter. This ignores, however, the long-established practice in some East Asian

---

[4] Tokyo, while a "city" in the broad sense, is in Japanese referred to with the character for metropolis/capital (都, *to*), and is one of Japan's forty-seven prefectures. It consists of numerous cities and wards and several subprefectures comprised of islands. Technically speaking, Kanda-Jinbōchō (神田神保町) is a district of Chiyoda Ward, but, as with many areas, is considered a distinct town by its inhabitants. It is often known just as Jinbōchō (or Jimbōchō, in an older romanization).

[5] Japanese bookstores often include *shoten* (書店, bookstore) in their names, even if they are a *furuhonya* (古本屋, used bookshop).

[6] Frank (2017), 21–23.

centers of neighborhoods being considered towns, with several historic book towns asserting their identity as such long before the modern use of the term in Europe, Kanda-Jinbōchō having done so since the early twentieth century.[7] Such towns are fundamentally associated with the book trade and are distinct from those associated with other cultural pursuits, such as music or theatre. By this broader metric, a book town might be described as a locale in which a cluster of businesses and institutions tied to books has developed to such an extent that the area becomes intrinsically identified with the book trade.[8] From this perspective, one can recognize Kanda-Jinbōchō as a book town without detracting from Hay-on-Wye's well-deserved recognition in leading the book town movement.[9]

Kanda-Jinbōchō enthusiastically promotes itself as *Hon no Machi* (本の街) – Book Town – a label deployed not only on signs and local souvenir maps but also on things like shopping bags (Figure 1). While the area by no means has a monopoly on print culture in the capital – Akihabara, the center of *otaku* (anime/manga/gaming fandom) culture, boasts an extraordinary collection of manga cafes and events selling fan-made manga, for example – nowhere else in Tokyo, or in Japan as a whole, is as strongly associated with books and reading as Kanda-Jinbōchō.[10] This is immediately apparent to anyone arriving there. Getting off the subway at Jimbōchō Station, located near the intersection of the town's two main streets, Yasukuni-dōri and Hakusan-dōri, one passes book-inspired designs and artwork to be met by racks of books for sale and advertisements for book-related events.

---

[7] Part of Kaifeng, China, was recognized as a book town by the late eighteenth century, and while the area promotes itself today to English-speaking tourists as the Street of Bookstores, the term in Chinese is 書店街 (Bookstore Town).

[8] This would also encompass towns strongly associated with the book trade in early modern Europe, such as Wittenberg (see Pettegree, 2010, 91–106).

[9] Alex Johnson, in his 2018 photo-essay book *Book Towns*, distinguishes between "official" and "unofficial" book towns, with Jinbōchō among the latter. For a comparative study of Kanda-Jinbōchō and Hay-on-Wye, see Ōuchi et al. (2008).

[10] Understandably, the town features heavily in works about used books and book collecting, such as Yagi (2007).

Figure 1 Paper shopping bag from a bookstore in Kanda-Jinbōchō, 2013. The text reads 神田　本の街 (*Kanda: Hon no Machi*, or Kanda: Book Town), with the 本 (*hon*, book) serving as a stylized map of the region.

The used bookstores are the primary draw, and collectively they constitute perhaps the largest used book market in the world.[11] There are nearly

---

[11] Another contender for the top position might have been College Street in Kolkata, India, although whether it will recover its former character after the destruction caused by Cyclone Amphan in May 2020 remains to be seen.

200, 130 of which comprise the Kanda Used Booksellers Federation (神田古書店連盟, Kanda Koshoten Renmei) and manage the town's "Book Town Jimbou" website (Figure 2), complete with downloadable reference maps and a searchable database for both stores and books. The site was overhauled in three languages to provide better online service in the wake of the coronavirus pandemic.

Moving along Yasukuni-dōri, one finds the majority of the bookstores located on the south side of the street, facing north to keep their wares out of the sun. As many stores have shelves and tables of wares that reach into the street, the entire sidewalk functions as one extended marketplace (Figure 3).[12] The north side does contain bookstores, but more of the space is occupied by cafes – many of which are book cafes offering reading material for perusal and purchase – and shops selling snacks to the book hunters slowly working their way through the area's offerings. Some degree of strategy is necessary: head straight to one's regular haunts, or pause to work through the pile of books a busy shopkeeper has just deposited on the sidewalk?

The used bookstores themselves, many independently owned and operated by the same families for generations, show a dynamic range. There are tiny one-room stores with treasures buried, often literally, under mountains of books so numerous that the pretense of shelving was all but abandoned long ago. Weaving around the roof-high piles, one has to avoid triggering a book-slide. Then there are the large, well-organized multistory establishments equipped with convenient counters and decorated with scrolls or

---

[12] As architectural scholar Alice Covatta (2017) observes,

> When in Jimbocho, visitors cannot fail to notice its peculiar type of "urban fabric" where almost every bookshop creates an outer extension and transforms the streets into a permanent marketplace. This outer extension creates a one-of-a-kind overturning because readers have an intimate feeling right in the middle of a traffic-congested arterial road. The described uncanny environment has developed behaviors, movements, traditions and rituality.

Figure 2 "Book Town Jimbou" website (http://jimbou.info), March 10, 2022.

Figure 3 Kanda-Jinbōchō, November 2020. Top: Yaguchi Shoten
(矢口書店), bottom: Nankaidō Shoten (南海堂書店).

beautiful *ukiyoe* art prints. Shops generally specialize in certain areas of study or literary genres, which are indicated on maps and pamphlets for the convenience of customers and booksellers alike.[13]

In addition to the used bookstores, the town contains some seventy bookstores selling new books, including the flagship stores of several major bookstore chains. There are also numerous libraries, several major universities with extensive collections such as Meiji University nearby, and a range of restaurants and cafes. It is common for both locals and those from out of town to make a day out of book-hunting in Kanda-Jinbōchō.

The town hosts a variety of literary events on a regular basis, such as readings, sessions with authors, and launch parties. There are also a range of events specifically celebrating reading and print culture, most prominently the annual Kanda Book Fair (Figure 4), which was first held in 1960. This week-long event, which takes place in the autumn, a season traditionally associated with reading in Japan, sees huge crowds milling among all the stalls put out by the bookstores from the moment the festival begins every morning.

Amidst all the bookstores, one may also notice various offices with posters advertising books. These are publishers. It should come as no surprise that the town is not only a site of the retail and consumption of books, but also of book production, for it is also the center of the Japanese publishing industry, hosting the head offices of many influential publishers, such as Iwanami Shoten, Shōgakukan, Shūeisha, and Yūhikaku, and branch offices of most of the rest.

In the wake of the devastating earthquake and tsunami that rocked northern Japan on March 11, 2011, Kanda-Jinbōchō became a site for the publishing industry's response to the disaster. While the town itself suffered only minimal damage, the publishing distribution network experienced setbacks and temporarily broke down in the northern region, where editors and volunteers struggled to carry in by hand newly printed books for victims of the disaster. Many publishers also suffered damage to their warehouses, large numbers of which

---

[13] For a current official map of the used bookstores in Kanda-Jinbōchō, see https://jimbou.info/map. In addition to locating bookstores, maps also assist those on literary pilgrimages by identifying related sites, such as the remains of the well of Kyokutei Bakin (曲亭馬琴, 1767–1848), a famous early modern author. For an analysis of such Kanda-Jinbōchō guide maps, see Taylor (2016).

Figure 4 The Kanda Book Fair (神田古本まつり, Kanda Furuhon Matsuri), October 2008.

were located in Chiba Prefecture to the east. While some warehouses were reinforced and only superficially damaged, this was not the case for all of them; moreover, even reinforced warehouses suffered damage when the earthquake triggered sprinkler systems, ruining large numbers of books and many pieces of equipment. Paper-manufacturing plants also suffered damage, with large stocks of paper and machinery rendered useless. The publishers gathered relief donations from the community, donated their own time and money to relief efforts, and worked to ensure a flow of reliable information.[14]

The publishers also worked to get back up to speed as soon as possible in order to publish what were to become the first of many, many books about the disaster. This was not only good business acumen, but also reflected a desire to help people come to terms with the disaster. Simultaneously, getting regular publishing back on schedule served to restore a sense of normalcy. In many ways this response had a precursor in the Great Kantō Earthquake of 1923, but unlike the recent disaster the prior one had a far more direct impact on Kanda-Jinbōchō. It nearly completely destroyed Kanda-Jinbōchō yet also ultimately cemented the town's position as the book center of Japan. In order to show how this occurred, it is first necessary for us to turn to the origins of this book town and see how it developed.[15]

2.2 The Birth of a Book Town

In the seventeenth century, Japan underwent a dramatic print revolution.[16] Carving techniques enabling effective multicolored printing by using

---

[14] A coalition of publishing associations started a website (www.shuppan-taisaku.jp) to cover the industry's response. For more on the industry's response to the disaster, see Kikuchi (2012), and, for a timeline of relevant events, see Nihon Zasshi Kyōkai (2012).

[15] For outlines of the town's history, see Wakimura (1979) and *Jinbōchō ga Suki da!* (2019). Author Shiba Ryōtarō has an account of the area (1995); for a more in-depth treatment, see Kashima (2017).

[16] While woodblock printing existed since ancient times, it was largely limited to temples throughout the medieval era. While moveable type technology existed, it failed to catch on (it lacked the flexibility of woodblocks for handling the various forms of Japanese text as well as combinations of image and text), resulting in a reversion to woodblocks.

multiple woodblocks transformed the art world, while the rise of commercial publishing fueled the specialization of each part of the publishing process.[17] The resulting development of mass-market printing put more books into more hands across the country than ever before. The greater range of works, and the accessibility thereof, was not without significant social ramifications. As Mary Elizabeth Berry has argued, the dawn of an increasingly shared print culture across the major cities of the time may have contributed to the emergence of a national Japanese identity.[18] While the city of Edo – present-day Tokyo – was fast becoming a major center for book production and retail, it was not yet the unparalleled locus of the publishing industry it would become by the dawn of the twentieth century.

Kanda-Jinbōchō, however, was not related to any facet of this flourishing print culture save consumption, for it certainly contained many educated readers. In the early modern era, the town was instead known for its numerous residences of *daimyō* (大名), the regional lords who comprised the warrior aristocracy. The *daimyō* were legally required to alternate between their home domains and Edo, the center of the *bakufu* (幕府, military government headed by a *shōgun*) regime – usually spending a year in each – as part of the administration's way of keeping an eye on them.[19] Of course, this required extensive residences in Edo, which needed to be maintained year-round because the wives and heirs of the *daimyō* were forced to stay there whenever the lords returned to their domains. We can gain some sense of the town by considering a map from the mid-nineteenth century when this was still the case (Figure 5).[20]

---

[17] See Kornicki (2001), 136–147, and Moretti (2020).

[18] Berry (2007). Moretti (2020), however, is skeptical about the extent to which this was the case (18–19).

[19] This requirement was known as the alternate attendance (参勤交代, *sankin kōtai*) system.

[20] For a look at how maps reveal the development of the town, see KANDA Renaissance Shuppanbu (1996), Toyama et al. (2018), and Toyama (2019).

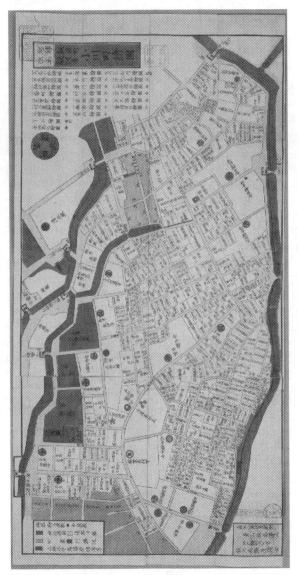

Figure 5 Today's Kanda-Jinbōchō as it was in the mid-nineteenth century. Circled are the Jinbō landholding and the adjoining alley (from Kageyama et al., 1849–1862).

At a glance we can discern a subdivision into larger and smaller areas: the former being *daimyō* residences and the latter residences of the *hatamoto* (旗本), or *bakufu* retainers. There are also various government facilities, firefighting locations, and so forth. The current name Kanda-Jinbōchō (lit. Kanda Jinbō Town) evolved from a combination of two elements, the first of which was the area becoming known as Kanda in 1872, when the capital was undergoing reorganization during Japan's modernization in the early Meiji era (1868–1912). It remained Kanda Ward until the capital was reorganized again in 1947 during postwar reconstruction, whereupon it became part of Chiyoda Ward but retained its former name unofficially. Jinbō, on the other hand, came from the Jinbō (神保) *hatamoto* family who had lived in the area.[21] Reflecting this origin, the design of a town council symbol is a *hatamoto*'s jacket (Figure 6).

How, then, did a town known for the residences of high-ranking samurai become a book town? Not long after the Meiji Restoration of 1868, when the new Japanese government embarked on a radical program of modernization, the samurai ceased to exist as a social class (although many ex-samurai continued to occupy significant roles in society). Most of the lords and their families returned to their home regions, leaving the buildings dormant. The small houses formerly occupied by retainers or *bakufu* offices became the homes of officials and a new generation of intellectuals, while the large *daimyō* residences were gradually replaced by institutions like hospitals, and, more than anything else, schools. This transformation was fueled by the expansion of the new education system: schools were nationalized and standardized in the early 1870s, with compulsory primary

---

[21] There is some debate over the precise connection between the area and its namesake family. One theory holds that it was named after Jinbō Hōkinokami (神保伯耆守, early to mid-nineteenth century), while another asserts that it arose from his ancestor Jinbō Nagaharu (神保長治, 1641–1715), but the name of the area appears to have arisen at some time in between these historical figures. The name may also have arisen from the family's land in the area, a government office established upon it, or the adjoining alley (see, for instance, "Tōkyō Kanda-Jinbōchō no Okori," 2020).

Figure 6 Kanda-Jinbōchō Third District Town Council sign in the shape of a *hatamoto*'s jacket. The sign briefly

education focusing on literacy, leading to rapid growth in the reading population.[22]

In and around Kanda-Jinbōchō, in addition to primary and secondary schools, institutions of higher learning were soon established. Tokyo University, founded in 1877 after a complex process of consolidating former *bakufu* educational institutions in the area, eventually settled in Hongō (today part of Bunkyō Ward) just to the north. The land had formerly been the residence of the powerful Maeda *daimyō* family of Kaga Domain, the famous Akamon (赤門, red gate) of which survives today as the university's main entrance. Over the subsequent decades, other universities founded in the vicinity included Hōsei, Meiji, and Nihon Universities, all of which were founded in 1920, Juntendō University (1946), and Ochanomizu University, Tokyo University of Science, and Kyōritsu Women's University (1949). Several of these evolved from older institutions: Juntendō University began as Japan's first modern hospital in 1838, Kyōritsu Women's University had its origin in a small women's school begun in 1886, and Nihon University was originally a law school founded in 1889. Over the years several universities located elsewhere also opened branch campuses in Kanda-Jinbōchō.

Nowhere else in Japan at the time compared to this center of higher learning in the capital, and elite students from across the country gathered in the area.[23] This, in turn, resulted in a drastic increase in the demand for books. Students needed specialized texts in medicine, law, science, and engineering, as well as in areas of social science such as economics and linguistics, particularly works in Western languages.[24] Such works were difficult to acquire and expensive, and while some university scholars could afford to invest in extensive book collections,

---

[22] On the evolution of modern Japanese education, see Yamazumi (1987) and Yamamoto (2014); on the development of universities in particular, see Amano (2009, 2016).

[23] See, for instance, Suzuki (1985), 71.

[24] Western texts were called *yōsho* (洋書). Translations from Western languages were not new (see Clements, 2015), but a broader range of languages and texts was involved and the scale was of a heretofore unforeseen magnitude.

students often lacked the space and financial means to follow suit. Instead, they sought easier and cheaper ways to gain these works, as well as a means of selling them when they were finished with them. This situation created a business opportunity in the area, particularly for former retainers and other residents who needed to seek out new livelihoods once the elite ex-samurai had departed. As a result, the number of bookstores in the area, particularly those specializing in various genres of used books, began to rapidly increase, a trend that only multiplied as the educated reading population soared into the dawn of the twentieth century.[25] The large number of secondhand bookstores in Kanda-Jinbōchō is evident from a map depicting the situation in 1903 (Figure 7).

The small black squares indicate a used bookstore (and several publishers), while the circles with the character 文 in them indicate schools.[26] Already by this date we can see many educational institutions surrounded by clusters of bookstores, illustrating how before Kanda-Jinbōchō was a book town, it was a school town, and it was the schools that fueled the boom in the area's book trade.[27]

2.3 Early Bookstores

The demand for books shot up at the same time that innovations in the Japanese book trade enabled it to rise to the challenge of effectively meeting that demand. Improved printing technology – first and foremost the introduction of industrial powered presses in the late nineteenth

---

[25] Examining map data makes the development particularly clear, as a wave of schools opening from the 1870s was followed by the arrival of many bookstores in the 1880s and 1890s, turning into a great torrent by the 1910s and 1920s (see Toyama, 2019).

[26] Buddhist swastikas on the map indicate religious institutions; the one on the far right is the famous Nikolai-do Orthodox Cathedral.

[27] Kanda-Jinbōchō was also known for cheap student housing (hence the pun *binbōchō*, or "poor town"), and continued to be until the 1960s. A popular view holds that it transitioned from a student town to a book town around that time, but in truth it began developing into a book town by the turn of the century. The students and books were hardly mutually exclusive; in fact, for much of the town's modern history, they fueled one another.

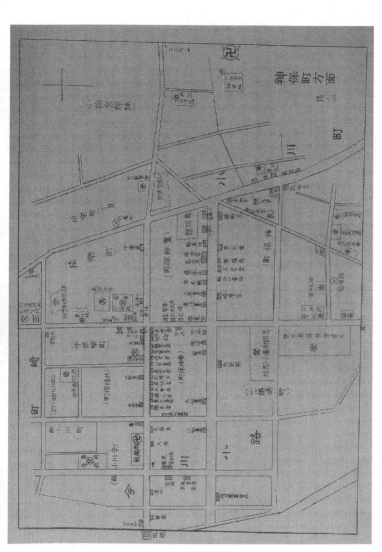

Figure 7 Map of used bookstores in Kanda-Jinbōchō, 1903 (from Tokyo Association of Dealers in Old Books, 1964).

century – drove down the price of print and distribution networks improved.[28] Instead of printing works themselves, publishers usually enlisted the services of specialized printers, which made the production of print material cheaper and more accessible than ever before. There were therefore fewer barriers to entering the publishing trade and soon both large-scale and small-scale publishers proliferated, striving to satisfy a growing educated urban class hungry for printed material. By the 1910s, Japan was experiencing a print culture boom that shaped urban life in a way heretofore unseen – newspapers and magazines multiplied, advertising grew, and women and children became increasingly larger readerships targeted by dedicated publications, all trends that continued to intensify through the 1920s.[29]

Understandably, bookstores proliferated and came to occupy a vital role in the cultural landscape of the era. As was the case in cities elsewhere in the world at the time, notably European centers but also prominent Asian cities like Shanghai, among educated urbanites, and most prominently students and intellectuals, regular visits to bookstores became a part of daily life.[30] Bookstores became increasingly important social spaces. This was because, while the primary function they served was the provision of intellectual sustenance and entertainment, many bookstores

---

[28] By the 1890s, high-speed printing machines manufactured by Marinoni were being used to print Japanese newspapers, for example. Woodblock printing continued, but came to be seen as an art form reserved for beautiful images and special purposes rather than as a viable method for regular mass printing. On distribution, see, for instance, Takahashi (1982).

[29] There is a plethora of scholarship on various aspects of Japanese print culture and evolving readerships from the late nineteenth century to the early twentieth. On newspapers, see, for example, Huffman (1997) and Akiyama (2002); on artistic prints, see Meech-Pekarik (1986); on women readers, see Frederick (2006), Patessio (2010), and Marshall (2019); on general-audience magazines see Nagamine (1997) and Satō (2002); on issues in literature and print culture, see Kawana (2018) and Shockey (2019); and on the reading public in general, see Nagamine (1997, 2004).

[30] As Leo Ou-Fan Lee (1999) notes, "For Shanghai writers the most important pastime, aside from going to the movies, was going to the bookstores" (120).

also served other roles specifically for the intellectual community. Some functioned as salons, providing vital social spaces for students and intellectuals to meet and socialize. These could serve a practical function, by connecting writers to colleagues and would-be publishers, for example, but in a more abstract sense they also represented spaces in which visitors could socially perform the role of intellectuals by engaging in activity and discussion that appropriately distinguished them.

Bookstores operated as nodes in the intellectual networks of the era, meaning visiting a bookstore was a way to directly participate in this culture. Because to read marked one as an intellectual, to be seen reading or engaged in tasks pertaining to reading – the perusal, purchase, and discussion of books – represented a type of social performance signaling others that you too were educated and sophisticated. Bookstore owners had an obvious incentive to embrace this association and play up their stores as intellectual spaces in order to attract a regular clientele. They were aided greatly in this endeavor if they were themselves intellectuals: at a time when being a merchant, including in the book trade, still carried unsavory associations, being recognized as a fellow intellectual by one's customers enabled one to sidestep some of the suspicion leveled at merchants. Customers would also be drawn to booksellers they knew as former colleagues, students, or teachers, ensuring that a merchant could count on people ready to buy their wares (and provide wares, if, like most of the shops in Kanda-Jinbōchō, the business dealt in used books).

Among all of the bookstores in Kanda-Jinbōchō, the oldest appears to be Takayama Honten (高山本店), founded in 1875. The founder had previously worked as a bowyer for a *daimyō*, who had departed and left his former employee without a job. The former bowyer, one surmises, assessed what business would be most needed in the area and opened a used bookstore. Takayama Honten remains open today, selling used books primarily in the areas of Japanese history, traditional theatre, and martial arts. In 1881, Hayashi Yūteki (早矢仕有的, 1837–1901) opened a used bookstore called Nakanishi-ya (中西屋) in order to sell to students remainders and damaged books that could not be moved at Maruzen (丸善), a major bookstore specializing in importing foreign books he had founded in Yokohama in 1869.[31] Nakanishi-ya later became an official branch of Maruzen.[32] Other notable bookstores that survive from that time include Sanseidō Shoten (三省堂書店, founded in 1881) and its longtime competitor Tōkyōdō Shoten (東京堂書店, founded in 1891), both of which sell new books. Sanseidō – today a chain comprising more than fifty stores throughout the country, with its crown a six-story building in Kanda-Jinbōchō stocking some 1.4 million volumes – was founded by the family of a *hatamoto* living near what is today Meiji University.[33] Clearly the phenomenon of former *hatamoto* turning to the book trade in the late nineteenth century was fairly common.

Another common phenomenon was that of bookstores evolving into publishers. Yūshikaku (有史閣) was the second bookstore to open in Kanda-Jinbōchō, being founded in 1877, two years after Takayama Honten.[34] Two years later, the bookstore, already becoming a popular

---

[31] A second Maruzen branch was opened in Nihonbashi (another area of Tokyo) in 1870. Hayashi was a student of the famous intellectual Fukuzawa Yukichi (福澤諭吉, 1835–1901). Maruzen was named for "Maruya Zenpachi," its reputed proprietor (invented by Hayashi as a gimmick). Hayashi is one of the people credited for the name of the "Hayashi rice" dish, but this cannot be confirmed. On Maruzen, see Maruzen Kabushiki-gaisha (1980), and Checkland (2003), 59–72.

[32] For more on Nakanishi-ya and its context, see Maruzen Kabushiki-gaisha (1980), 82–96, and Ōuchi (2009), 12–23.

[33] Sanseidō was originally a *geta* (wooden sandals) shop but after a fire reemerged as a bookstore. Kamei Makiko, the wife of founder Kamei Tadakazu, intensely studied German, English, and French to help handle foreign texts (Suzuki, 1985, 70). For more on Sanseidō, see Sanseidō Shoten Hyakunen-shi Kankō Iinkai (1981).

[34] However, it is often incorrectly regarded as the first, perhaps because of its later fame as a publisher. The proprietors, Egusa Onotarō (江草斧太郎, 1857–1908) and his wife, embraced their store's role as a salon for local students and became parental figures who looked after them, lent them money, and so on (Suzuki, 1985, 46). A similar case of a bookstore salon focused primarily on students was Nishikawa Seikōdō (西川誠光堂) in Kyōto (see Matsuki, 1986). The bookstore

hangout for students, changed its name to Yūhikaku (有斐閣) and entered the publishing trade as well – today it is one of Japan's most well-known publishers. Other examples of businesses in Kanda-Jinbōchō starting out as bookstores and evolving into publishers include the aforementioned Sanseidō (which entered the publishing industry in 1884) and Nakanishi-ya (1887).[35] The most famous example, however, is no doubt the well-known publisher of literary classics and scholarly monographs, Iwanami Shoten (岩波書店).

Iwanami Shoten was founded as a used bookstore in 1913 by Iwanami Shigeo (岩波茂雄, 1881–1946), but only a year later it came to national attention by publishing the landmark novel *Kokoro* (こゝろ, *Heart*) by Shigeo's mentor, the literary giant Natsume Sōseki (夏目漱石, 1867–1916).[36] Iwanami Shoten's case illustrates well the importance of intellectual networking, especially in the highbrow book trade. Shigeo had been living in Kanda-Jinbōchō since his student days, marrying the daughter of the household where he had been rooming, but it was through his network that he made his mark on the area. Through his friends, he was able to rent a shop space and supply it with used books to sell.[37] His close friends, especially the intellectuals Abe Yoshishige and Abe Jirō, were, along with Shigeo, all members of the Mokuyōkai (木曜会, Thursday Society), a collection of Sōseki's disciples and various visitors who met at their

salons of Kanda-Jinbōchō would made an interesting comparison to similar institutions elsewhere at the end of the nineteenth century to the early twentieth, such as Sylvia Beach's Shakespeare and Company in Paris (see Beach, 1959; Fitch, 1983), or Uchiyama Kanzō's Uchiyama Shoten in Shanghai (see Uchiyama, 1960; Keaveney, 2009; Kato, 2022).

[35] Further north, a notable example is Kanehara Shuppan (金原出版), which started as a pawn shop called Kanehara Isekiten (金原医籍店) near Tokyo University in 1875, evolved into a book shop by 1878 when the owner noted the demand for texts among medical students, and had become a publisher by 1881 (Suzuki, 1985, 22–24). It remains a respected publisher of medical texts.

[36] On Iwanami Shigeo and his publishing house, see Abe (1957), Iwanami Shoten (1996), Kōno (2013), and Nakajima (2013).

[37] See, for example, Wakimura (1979), 136, and Kōno (2013), 37. Accepting donated books from friends was a fairly common way to build a used bookseller's initial inventory.

mentor's residence most Thursdays.[38] As an intellectual himself, Shigeo enjoyed the trust and support of his colleagues, who became his suppliers and customers, and later also authors and editors once he entered publishing. The most significant figure in this regard was Sōseki himself, who not only lent Shigeo funds, but, more importantly, bestowed cultural capital upon his disciple's enterprise in two ways.

First, he provided the calligraphic sign for the store – something even the press took note of – which was significant because it represented an endorsement from a position of intellectual authority at a time when publishers had to navigate a minefield of presumed conflicts between commercial and cultural commitments.[39] Second, by agreeing to the publication of *Kokoro* – which, having just finished a successful run in serial format in the *Asahi Shinbun* newspaper, was a guaranteed bestseller as a single-volume edition – he was ensuring Iwanami Shoten would become well known among the literati as a whole, as well as bringing it much-needed capital.[40] Iwanami Shoten went on to influence Japanese publishing as a whole, shaping literary canons, pioneering the concept of set prices for books, and introducing the *bunkobon* (文庫本, 105 x 148 mm) and *shinshobon* (新書本, normally 103 x 182 mm) book formats that are industry standards today.[41]

---

[38] The Mokuyōkai functioned as a loosely organized salon, first arranged by one of Sōseki's disciples to handle the many people eager to meet Sōseki, while conveniently setting up the disciples as gatekeepers.

[39] See, for instance, *Tōkyō Asahi Shinbun*, September 12, 1913. The original sign was destroyed in the 1923 conflagration, but the imprint survived and is still used by Iwanami Shoten. The relationship between commerce and culture is, of course, a major concern among scholars of print culture. On this aspect of Sōseki's support for Iwanami, see, for instance, Kōno (2013), 40.

[40] Much modern literature in the late Meiji era was initially published in serial format and then republished in volume format if it proved successful. *Kokoro* – often regarded as Iwanami's first publication, but actually his third – represented both substantial income and immense cultural capital, and put Iwanami on the map in the publishing world.

[41] Regarding set prices (正札販売, *shōfuta hanbai*) for merchandise, department stores had been introducing these by the end of the nineteenth century, but in bookstores, as in much of the Japanese retail world at the time, pricing schemes

Iwanami Shoten represents a spectacularly successful case of a bookstore transitioning into a publisher, but as the other examples indicate, it was not unique. Certainly, such transitions were most successful when the bookstore owner was proficient at networking and had an established clientele with particular tastes that they could target with publications. As readers in the book trade will be well aware, operating a bookstore enables one to gain considerable insight into the book market: what type of works are in demand, how many are needed in stock, and what prices are most suitable. It is a trade well suited to developing a good eye for books. Conversely, if one wishes to gain experience dealing with books and readers before plunging into the world of publishing, getting one's feet wet in dealing books is one reasonable way to start. No doubt this helps explain why Kanda-Jinbōchō, gaining fame for its used bookstores, also gave birth to numerous leading publishers around the same time.[42]

Of course, not every publisher followed this path. The most notable exception was Noma Seiji (野間清治, 1878–1938), a staff member at Tokyo Imperial University who had recruited students from a debate

---

were expected to vary by customer and time, and haggling was routine. Iwanami Shigeo was no doubt one of the first book merchants to implement set prices and contributed to its spread among bookstores, but while often credited for the innovation (e.g., Abe, 1957, 123; Iwanami Shoten, 1996, 3), he appears to have gleaned the idea from Nakamura-ya (中村屋), a bakery run by the Sōma couple, Aizō and Tokko (who used the term "regular price" (正価販売, *seika hanbai*), although the meaning was identical; see Sōma, 1938, 56–59). As bookstores and publishers increasingly adopted set price policies, there was an impetus to build a shared system, eventually leading to the current convention of printing prices directly on books.

[42] English websites discussing Kanda-Jinbōchō often credit Iwanami with establishing the town as a book town, which is putting the cart before the horse: Iwanami Shigeo opened his store in the town because it was already an established book town, not the other way around. These sites all appear to be taking their information from Wikipedia, which also used to ("Jinbōchō, Tokyo," October 21, 2020) contain various errors such as identifying Iwanami Shigeo as a university professor (he was a former teacher but never a professor, and had no graduate degrees).

society to publish a magazine entitled *Yūben* (雄辯, *Eloquence*). When he failed to find any publishers willing to take on the project, he took it on himself after convincing one of the major printing companies to help. Eventually his operation merged with the debate society proper and published a journal called *Kōdan Kurabu* (講談倶楽部, *Story Club*), from which the publishing outfit took the name Kōdansha (講談社, founded proper in 1909). By the late 1920s, it had risen to the top of the publishing world, and it remains Japan's largest publisher today.[43]

The boom in bookstores and publishers in Kanda-Jinbōchō was further sustained by cultural developments in the wake of the First World War. The Taishō era (1912–1926) was a time of government transition, popular political movements, and social upheaval, as well as a booming print culture that enabled people to engage with, critique, or satirize these developments. Intellectual movements that seized the public imagination also played a role because they accorded reading a vital role in both personal and social development. The "philosophy boom" (哲学ブーム, *tetsugaku būmu*) that took off around 1920 saw philosophy books become essential commodities for any educated urbanite; introductory texts to the subject exploded while parents, fearful of their children being left behind and believing philosophy offered the key to Japan's progress as a modern nation, demanded philosophy classes at their schools. In contrast to how today philosophy tends to be dismissed as useless by mainstream society, during the 1920s it enjoyed popular support, with logic and critical inquiry seen as highly practical skills – at least in principle (young pupils forced to grapple with Hegel and Schopenhauer might have had other ideas).

A related but much more enduring intellectual development was the *Kyōyōshugi* (教養主義) movement, which had its roots in the turn of the century but was in full swing in the early 1920s. *Kyōyōshugi*, a term that spread from a translation for *bildungsroman* (教養小説, *kyōyō shosetsu*), came to refer to a form of self-cultivation that was bound up with the experience of reading and discussing literary classics.[44] Reading as a means

---

[43] On Kōdansha, see Itō (1994) and Marshall (2019), 47–76.

[44] *Kyōyō*, the root of the term, is used to refer to intellectual or cultural cultivation and is synonymous with liberal arts in Japanese educational institutions.

to develop one's character was hardly a new concept in Japan, but traditional self-cultivation among the literati had generally been associated with mastery of the classical Confucian canon. Japanese literature and thought had certainly been long valued and celebrated, but for their aesthetic qualities and cultural values rather than as a means to perfect the self. *Kyōyōshugi*, on the other hand, was far more inclusive, reaching across barriers both temporal and spatial – the new canons included works both ancient and modern, Japanese and foreign, and the very consideration of aesthetic or psychological aspects was held up as just as meaningful for self-cultivation as the study of ethics.[45] There was an element of elitism – one needed time and money to invest in reading and discussion of a large body of works, for one thing – but it was not the elitism of old, for in the *Kyōyōshugi* mold it was one's knowledge and sophistication that marked a true modern citizen, not wealth or family background.

The upshot of the philosophy boom and the *Kyōyōshugi* movement was the establishment of reading as a moral imperative for modern citizens at a time when more of them could read than ever before. Only the well-read would possess the thinking skills necessary to shape the destiny of their communities and ultimately the nation. No longer, ran the idealistic thinking, was this destiny merely in the hands of a small group of nobles or scholars – the doors had been thrown open to all and it was the duty of the entire population to take up this responsibility. The notion that reading was fundamental to the building of character, and that this betterment of the self was not only a way to access future opportunities but also to contribute to society, endured as a pillar of the Japanese education system into the 1970s and echoes down to the present.

---

[45] In the postwar era, *Kyōyōshugi* suffered from its portrayal as indulgent naval-gazing by intellectuals like Maruyama Masao and Karaki Junzō motivated to critique many of their prewar forbears for their perceived failure to stand up to militarism. This was a caricature of prewar intellectuals, but it proved surprisingly enduring until the early 2000s when a new generation of scholars revisited the topic and ushered in in-depth studies of the topic (first and foremost Takeuchi Yō, see 2003 and 2018).

Because it had become vital for everyone to read, the act of reading in public became normalized, widespread, and even fetishized. Reading on the train on one's daily commute or during lunch became a default social expectation rather than just a way to pass the time. As reading became associated with sophistication while simultaneously becoming an expected social act irrespective of one's class, occupation or location, the book trade was quick to move to capitalize on these developments, building influential reputations and immense profit through offering reading material – and with it, cultural capital. When in 1927 Iwanami Shoten launched its Iwanami Bunko series of classic pocketbooks, inspired by the German Reclams Universal Bibliotek, the publisher captured the spirit of the moment in a short text included near the back of every volume:

> In order to make people ignorant, the liberal arts have been closed [off from them] in narrow halls. There is now a truly serious demand from progressives to take back wisdom and beauty from their monopol[ization] by the elite class . . . Taking as a model Reclams, [we will] publish . . . many "must-read" books . . . that truly have value as classics . . . and offer materials for the necessary life-advancement of every human being.[46]

The increasing value of books as status symbols, especially among the growing urban middle class, dovetailed with a rising interest in books as art objects and the development of new techniques in book design and illustration. The simple covers devoid of illustration that were typical of early modern books gave way to beautiful designs meant to entice customers and be shown off. The social display of reading habits extended into the home, with decorative bookcases becoming popular – a trend some publishers seized upon when they offered attractive bookcases as free incentives for readers to subscribe to their respective collection of literary classics.[47]

---

[46] Iwanami (1927). On Iwanami Bunko, see Shockey (2019), 59–90.

[47] See, for instance, Mack (2010), 120–124, and Kawana (2018), 32–37. Subscription systems where readers paid a publisher in advance for a book or a series were common, but the risk this entailed for readers meant effective marketing was key.

The cultural capital accrued by some publishing brands gave rise to distinct subcultures: by the late 1920s, Iwanami Shoten had become so popular among students that they would carry around Iwanami books as fashion accessories, leading to them being labelled "Iwanami boys" and "Iwanami girls" (in parody of the labels of trendy leftist students as "Marx boys" and "Engels girls").

So it was that the book merchants in Kanda-Jinbōchō served a multiplicity of roles, providing intellectual nourishment in the form of print and socialization, and even in some cases serving as a form of subcultural identification. Book merchants in general benefited as reading became understood as the hallmark of a modern society, and bookstores as modernity's hubs: vital social spaces that linked intellectuals and regular readers, aged and youth, and people from different parts of the country who found in bookstores a shared community. It was a good time to be in the book trade, and Kanda-Jinbōchō, already recognized as Tokyo's book town, was right in the center. It was at this precise historical juncture that the book town – along with most of the capital region – was all but obliterated.

2.4 Kanda-Jinbōchō in Crisis: The Great Kantō Earthquake

The social elements that shaped space in Kanda-Jinbōchō – people hunting down books for collections, meeting with friends to browse, reading or discussing books at cafes, and so forth – were already established by the turn of the century, but were reinforced by the cultural emphasis on reading in the 1920s. However, while the town became increasingly dominated by bookstores and publishers, several developments had also brought about structural changes in its broader spatial configuration. One was the arrival of streetcars around 1908, enabled by the expansion of the municipal electrical grid. Another was a major fire that tore through the town in February 1913, laying waste to many stores that were then replaced with more modern architecture, considerably changing the feel of the town. Iwanami Shoten, in fact, opened its doors on a plot destroyed in the fire. A map of the town in 1921 (Figure 8) reveals a well-structured town arranged in blocks, with many of the aforementioned stores, like Sanseidō and Takayama Shoten, in essentially the same locations they occupy today.

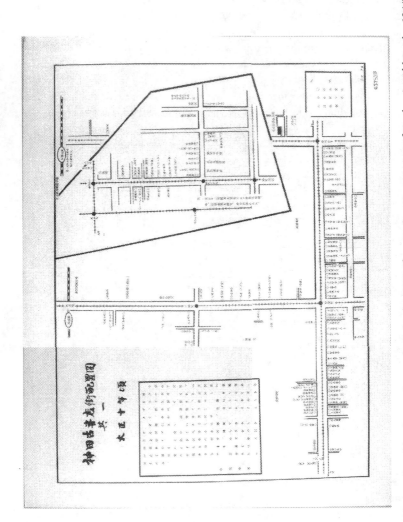

Figure 8 Map of used bookstores in Kanda-Jinbōchō, 1921 (from Tokyo Association of Dealers in Old Books, 1964).

By far the single greatest event that affected the town was the Great Kantō Earthquake. The earthquake, which struck just before noon on September 1, 1923, was a terrifying shock of magnitude 7.9, followed by a conflagration that reduced most of the greater Tokyo area to ashes. It traumatized a population caught in tight living quarters with no warning. Because much of the population had been preparing meals on small home stoves knocked over by the quake, fires broke out and spread rapidly, the flames fanned by typhoon winds. Total panic ensued, with people desperately trying to escape with their belongings, burning alive on congested roads or in buildings meant to protect them.[48] The books and paper stocks that formed the cornerstone of Kanda-Jinbōchō's intellectual and economic world were easy prey for the fires. Even newer buildings with brick construction became ovens, leaving pitiful skeletons dotting a blasted landscape. Bookstore owners despaired as they tried, usually in vain, to save precious volumes, while in nearby Hongō Ward Tokyo University's library caught fire and was all but wiped out.[49] It took three days to extinguish the fires. The Great Kantō Earthquake had reduced Tokyo's book town to ashes in the wind.

The initial response of those in the book trade was utter despair. The bookstores were simply gone while most major publishers saw their offices, stock, and much of their staff wiped out.[50] Resuming regular publication was impossible: "Magazines Annihilated / Almost Nothing to Come Out in October / Great Blow to Print Culture," proclaimed one Ōsaka headline.[51] The number of books lost ran into the millions. Residents of Kanda-Jinbōchō who had survived bemoaned the instantaneous destruction of the heart of Japanese print culture and the possibly irreparable damage to Japan's cultural

[48] Total casualties were more than 105,000 dead or missing, with more than 300,000 residences destroyed (Moroi and Takemura, 2004, 34).

[49] In a heartbreaking loss, only a tiny fraction of the library holdings could be saved, with some 760,000 volumes lost, many of which were rare and irreplaceable (Tōkyō Teikoku Daigaku, 1932, vol. 2, 1116–1117).

[50] On the impact of the damage on the area and the book trade, see Mack (2010), 51–89.

[51] *Ōsaka Asahi Shinbun*, September 8, 1923.

heritage this represented. There was talk among publishers about whether it might be better to abandon the ruins and start over in Osaka or Kyoto, while many booksellers left town or changed professions.[52]

However, Kanda-Jinbōchō defied expectations almost immediately. Bookstore owners called in connections to acquire books from elsewhere quickly, in some cases acquiring the collections of the same former samurai families who used to dwell in the area. They cleared areas and erected tents and stalls to renew selling books even while reconstruction efforts were underway. In addition to their established social networks, the bookstore owners had the benefit of the town's established reputation as a book town. Amidst the rubble and repair work, swarms of people from across the greater Kantō region came to the town seeking to replace libraries they had lost to the earthquake and fires.[53] The intense and immediate demand for books, directed squarely at the town, gave local bookstore owners a considerable advantage over their competitors elsewhere in Tokyo, who had to weigh reconstruction costs against uncertain demand. Booksellers outside Tokyo sold large collections to visitors from Kanda-Jinbōchō, considering this a good deal – until they realized the visitors were bookstore owners themselves who had promptly taken the books back to the town and sold them at a markup. Large amounts of money also flowed into Kanda-Jinbōchō from universities and the government, which needed to replace extensive lost collections and like private buyers counted on the town to meet their needs. The town's indelible association with the book trade and the plucky spirit of the merchants had saved it. It is no surprise that many stores were rebuilt in the same locations they had occupied beforehand: after all, everyone knew where they were and the customers had never stopped coming.

Publishers also played a role in renewing Kanda-Jinbōchō, and in turn benefited from the same demand for books that fueled the bookstores. In the case of Kōdansha, the disaster enabled the publisher to gain a position of

---

[52] Bookseller comments included "Because [running] a bookstore was no good anymore, I made it a dry goods store," and "I was doing this for a long time as well myself, but now I decided to change careers" (Hashimoto, 1964, 297).

[53] On the reconstruction of Tokyo after the disaster, see Schencking (2013).

influence that ultimately led to it dominating the publishing industry in a way inconceivable before the disaster. Founder Noma Seiji called on his company to stand up and respond to the disaster to show the populace that Japan's publishers were down but not out. In pursuing his plans, Noma had more options than other major publishers because Kōdansha's offices and equipment had been far less damaged. Having put the bread-and-butter business of magazines on hiatus for a month, Noma and his surviving employees decided to put what precious resources they had left to work on a special book about the disaster. The work required great improvisation as editors became reporters, broken houses were turned into makeshift workplaces, and textbook-grade paper obtained from a ship in Yokohama that had just arrived was adapted for the printing.[54]

The work, *Taishō Daishinsai Daikasai* (大正大震災大火災, *The Great Taishō Earthquake and Conflagration*), published on October 1 one month after the disaster, was only the second book about the earthquake to be published.[55] Unlike the first one, however, which was a rush job with little real content, Kōdansha's was a labor of love filled with descriptions, news, witness accounts, and personal reflections, as well as inspiration for a populace coming to terms with the disaster. It was filled with images, including artwork and a large number of reproduced photographs. It also contained what might strike some as inappropriate elements such as humor, suggestions on new business opportunities in the wake of the disaster, and even advertisements for other books, but these all contributed to a feeling of a return to normalcy. The book became a major bestseller overnight, but more important than the money it brought the publisher and the recovering bookstores throughout Kanda-Jinbōchō was the work's great effect at calming public anxiety. People spoke of how reading it helped them come to terms with the disaster, leaving them with the sense that Tokyo would be all right.[56] The book quickly sold all 400,000 copies, became famous across

---

[54] The paper had been imported for a rival publisher that, being in no condition to use it, allowed Kōdansha to have it.

[55] For more on Kōdansha's book, see Kurita (1968), 189–204, and Mack (2010), 72–76.

[56] See Hashimoto (1964), 295.

the country, and turned Kōdansha into a household name.[57] By the late
1920s, with the one-yen book (円本, *enpon*) phenomenon driving down
book prices and generating great amounts of stock that drew ever larger and
more diverse crowds to used booksellers, the town was thriving again
(Figure 9).[58]

So it was that, confounding fears that the Great Kantō Earthquake would
halt the rise of Kanda-Jinbōchō as not just a book town but also as a center
of Japanese print culture, in the wake of the disaster the town entered
a renaissance, its status secure. In contrast to the devastation wrought in
1923, Kanda-Jinbōchō suffered much less than much of Tokyo during the
US firebombing of the capital near the end of the Pacific War, giving rise to
the myth that perhaps "Japan hands" advising the United States, like Serge
Elisséeff (1889–1975) or Edwin O. Reischauer (1910–1990), had
intervened.[59] While fanciful, the notion revealed residents' confidence in
the town's reputation as a vital cultural center.[60]

2.5 An Established Book Town

Postwar reconstruction saw much demand for books, again to replace lost
collections. Following the 1949 educational reform, schools desiring accred-
itation as universities rushed to build sufficient library holdings to meet the
official criteria: since it was the numbers of volumes that mattered, not the
content, Kanda-Jinbōchō sellers could unload almost anything. Some
unscrupulous schools apparently borrowed large numbers of books from

---

[57] See Itō (1994), 58–60.

[58] On the one-yen book trend, usually understood as having been begun by the
publisher Kaizōsha (改造社) in 1926, see Ishizuka (1998), Shiobara (2002), and
Kawana (2018), 17–48.

[59] Elisséeff (or Eliseyev; Russian: Елисеев), an early Western Japanologist,
reputedly frequented Kanda-Jinbōchō for books while studying at Tokyo
University from 1908. Reischauer, born and raised in Tokyo, later studied
under him at Harvard.

[60] The notion seemed not entirely implausible given the real debates in the United
States over bombing targets and the efforts by some to spare Kyoto from
devastation.

Figure 9 Kanda-Jinbōchō in February 1934.

the used bookstores and returned them once government inspectors left. With everything "new" being in vogue during the 1950s, Kanda-Jinbōchō was put in the position of convincing the populace to keep buying used books, and the Book Fair, mentioned earlier, first began in 1960 as one response to the situation. Originally small in scale, it proved a tremendous success and grew with each successive year.[61] This, in turn, attracted to the town yet more businesses in the book trade, as well as increased attention nationwide, ushering in a new era of prosperity for the town. The student population of the area, already in decline, dropped substantially in the wake of the 1968 protest movement, but by that point the town's patrons had diversified and the bookstores no longer depended primarily upon student purchases.

Kanda-Jinbōchō was not born as a book town. Rather, its special place in the Japanese cultural milieu is a product of evolution over the course of the late nineteenth and early twentieth centuries from a samurai residential area to a school town and finally a book town in a natural progression of elements that was in turn fueled by human ingenuity. Its greatest challenge saw the town experience near-total annihilation, only to be reborn from the ashes all the stronger. It remains a manifest symbol of Japanese books and print culture in the face of contemporary challenges including online retailing, digitization, and the coronavirus pandemic that will be touched on in the following chapters. Let us now turn to consider how public reading spaces have evolved in the course of Japan's modern experience.

[61] Originally it occupied only a small area in a vacant lot near the Iwanami Jinbōchō Building and the organizers had trouble obtaining police permission to open the stalls.

3 The Ongoing Transformation of Public Reading Spaces

The story of reading spaces in modern Japan is one of both expansion and transformation. While the previous chapter focused on Kanda-Jinbōchō to outline the significance of bookstores in the late nineteenth and early twentieth centuries, the present one widens the scope to consider the evolution of public reading spaces. As readership expanded and reading practices evolved, so too did public reading spaces grow and change in response, modifying their institutional and/or spatial organization.

Bookstores are naturally places of commerce, but they also represent important spaces for readers – and reading, whether browsing in front of a shelf or enjoying a book in a dedicated area – within their communities. Of course, libraries and reading rooms or cafes are other key public reading spaces, ones with which this chapter will be particularly concerned. In this way, I am conceptualizing public reading spaces here not in the more limited sense of spaces managed by state actors, but in the more inclusive sense of communal spaces made open to people for reading and reading-related activities. Such spaces constitute one type of what the sociologist Ray Oldenburg conceptualized as "third places," those spaces distinct from one's home and work spaces and that play significant roles in building community.[62] This chapter will trace the evolution of these key reading spaces in modern Japan in relation to changing reading practices and the social context, from the late Edo era until contemporary times.

3.1 Early Modern Legacies

The print revolution that transformed the Edo period, coupled with rising literacy, particularly in urban areas, led to great amounts of books circulating.[63] This, in turn, fueled the practice of book collecting, which

---

[62] Oldenburg (1997). For an outline of books in early modern Japan, see Smith (1994), and for an in-depth overview, see Kornicki (2001).

[63] *Terakoya* (寺子屋, local private schools offering rudimentary education) are conventionally regarded as having played a significant role in commoner literacy. For an overview of the structure of Edo printed books, see Hioki (2009).

itself gave rise to expanding knowledge networks across the country.[64] Urban centers contained various types of bookstores, and peddlers would offer books on their rounds among neighborhoods or as they traveled along routes to smaller towns (Figure 10).[65] Personal libraries were usually small and owners reread books frequently and exchanged them with friends and family. This fit well within the classical traditions of education, which emphasized familiarity with a limited canon and committing extended passages to memory. Scholarly courtiers or particularly wealthy merchants, however, could possess large collections that represented a boon to scholarship if they made them available.

How did people read at the time? While a plethora of reading practices had evolved by the Edo era, one distinguishing characteristic was the persistence of an element of orality: many texts were read aloud (音読, *ondoku*), and were even written with this form of reading in mind. This, in turn, was bound up with reading as a social activity, where people read together and often aloud to one another. To some extent this may have been rooted in reading as ritual performance, dating back to the Nara and Heian eras when Buddhist sutras or Chinese classics were read aloud with reverence. In a related vein, reading aloud as a type of study, particularly in the form of commenting on a text (a form of reading called 講読, *kōdoku*) endured into the modern era. However, reading aloud with others was more often than not done for reasons of recreation and sociability: even by the late Heian period reading aloud was being performed for enjoyment with all manner of texts. Private reading, as well as silent reading alone or in groups (a practice that remained widespread in the postwar era, as we shall see), certainly existed as well, but reading aloud had several distinct advantages.

[64] On book collecting and networks, see Okamura (1996) and Shindō (2017), and on book collecting and its role in local knowledge in particular, see Kudō (2011).

[65] The dual-role publisher–bookseller was the typical model of the day. On early modern bookselling, see Konta (1977/2009), Suzuki (1980), and Moretti (2020). Inoue (1981) provides an exhaustive list of publishers. In the seventeenth century, Kyoto was foremost in publishing (with nearly three times as many publishers as Edo), but Osaka and Edo soon caught up, and by the nineteenth century, Edo had nearly twice as many publishers as Kyoto (Inoue, 1981, 5).

Figure 10 A late Edo-era bookstore. This one belonged to Araki Ihē (荒木伊兵衛) in the Shinsaibashi district of Osaka. Single-sheet print from the end of the Edo era or the start of Meiji (from the collection of Hashiguchi Kōnosuke / Seishindō Shoten).

It was helpful when not everyone was literate (while giving anyone versed in traditional storytelling a chance to show off), it was practical if books were particularly expensive to buy and the time borrowing them was limited, and most importantly it was a way to bond and enjoy a work together. In this way reading was just as often, if not more so, a public activity as a private one.[66]

As Peter Kornicki notes, reading was also transformed in the wake of the commercialization of the book trade that by the end of the seventeenth century had rendered books a commodity, posing a risk to the reverent attitude toward books and reading. This was a source of consternation for intellectuals like Kaibara Ekiken (貝原益軒, 1630–1714), troubled by a fear that thorough, respectful reading for self-enlightenment had been replaced by superficial, casual reading for entertainment.[67] A ritualized, respectful approach to reading (of the classics, naturally) persisted as an ideal, but was no longer descriptive of lived reality for most readers. At the same time, commercialization brought with it new forms of reading, such as the *yomiuri* (読売) who hawked news broadsheets (瓦版, *kawaraban*) and other publications through performative reading of them on the street, often in song and sometimes with musical accompaniment.[68]

In short, reading in early modern Japan most certainly had a public character, whether seen in the popular forms of shared reading and reading aloud, or in the selling of reading material through colorful public performance. Was there, however, anything yet analogous to public libraries? After all, while it was certainly no longer the case that only elites had regular access to reading material, purchasing books was often impractical for most families, lacking as they did either sufficient financial means (even an entertainment book could cost as much as several weeks' worth of food) or storage space to acquire many. While the lending and borrowing of

---

[66] On group reading in the Edo era, especially among intellectuals, see Maeda (2018).

[67] Kornicki (2001), 258–262. In Kornicki's words, with the advent of commercialization, "The printed page was not any longer so precious that one refrained from using it as toilet paper" (262).

[68] On the *yomiuri*, see Groemer (1994).

books among individual collectors dramatically grew during the period, those able to do so were the most likely to be able to afford collections themselves. The popular image is that libraries remained the purview of elites – and up until the latter half of the seventeenth century there was some truth to this. Libraries in premodern Japan largely came in three forms: those established or managed by the court or its ministries, those attached to temples and intended primarily to safeguard scripture, and those kept by the great courtier, and later warrior, families.[69] After these came libraries attached to schools and those held by individuals. Collections usually reflected individual curators' interests, lacked any consistent organization, and were not designed to facilitate access. Due to the time and cost involved in producing books, lending was a difficult proposition and not usually permitted by the institutional libraries.

The early modern era witnessed larger and better-organized institutional libraries, like the Gobunko (御文庫, later 紅葉山文庫 Momijiyama Bunko) begun by the first Edo *shōgun*, Tokugawa Ieyasu (徳川家康, 1543–1616), which eventually evolved to become part of today's National Archives. Such libraries, however, like the increasingly larger libraries established at schools and the reading rooms at major temples, remained inaccessible to the general public. Options did, though, expand as the period wore on.[70] Some of the domain libraries (attached to official domain schools) were open to the public, and while most only permitted reading on the premises, some allowed locals to borrow books. Fukuoka Domain apparently built a library specifically for public use in 1818, but shut it down

---

[69] The first state library was likely the Zushoryō (図書寮), founded at the dawn of the eighth century. While most of the great premodern collections were lost, almost always to fire, parts of some are extant – notably Kanazawa Bunko (金沢文庫), begun by the Hōjō family in the late thirteenth century, and the library of the Ashikaga Gakkō (足利学校), likely begun in the early fifteenth, which are considered two great centers of medieval learning. On premodern libraries, see Kornicki (2001), 364–376 for an overview, and for an in-depth look, see Shindō (2019), 11–152.

[70] On libraries in the Edo period, see Kornicki (2001), 376–397, and especially Shindō (2017, 2019, 153–238).

after locals began neglecting their work to spend all their time at the library.[71] One influential library was the Hada Hachimangū Bunko (羽田八幡宮文庫), attached to the Hada Hachimangū Shrine in what is today Toyohashi in Aichi Prefecture. The institution was intended for Shintō study but was open to scholars and townspeople alike, including visitors from out of town. With a set system of lending books – one signed a document promising to return a book within a month, replace it if it was damaged, and so forth – and dedicated space for reading, it represents a sort of forerunner of the modern library system.[72] The library was not always quiet: libraries hosted special events if a famous scholar or important official visited, with lectures and parties, which represented an important opportunity for local networking.[73] At the local level, many village heads also made their collections available to their fellow villagers, forming institutions often called *zōsho no ie* (蔵書の家) that served as important resources for locals.[74] Indeed, as the historian Shindō Tōru argues, the role of libraries in the late Edo period was not just the preservation of books, but increasingly also the provision of information resources for a more literate population.[75]

By far the most accessible source of reading material were the *kashihonya* (貸本屋) commercial lending libraries, the overwhelming majority of which took the form of peddlers who carried their collections around a circuit of neighborhoods and lent books for a fraction of the cost of buying them (Figure 11).[76] These merchants existed from the mid-seventeenth century but by the early nineteenth had become both specialized and widespread across the country.

While *kashihonya* offered everything from scholarship to erotica, their bread and butter was contemporary serial fiction, which often spanned many volumes over years. In this regard they were so successful that, by the early nineteenth century, the writers and publishers of such fiction had come to depend upon the *kashihonya* as a distribution network. More than any other force, the *kashihonya* enabled the early modern public to readily

---

[71] Kornicki (2001), 390. [72] Shindō (2019), 204–213. [73] Shindō (2019), 212–213.

[74] For more on these, see Kobayashi (1991). [75] Kobayashi (1991), 234.

[76] On *kashihonya*, see in particular Nagatomo's landmark study (1982).

Figure 11 An Edo-era *kashihonya*, as portrayed by the actor Yamashita Kinsaku I (初代山下金作), by the artist Nishimura Shigenaga (西村重長) in 1725.

access a larger amount and a wider range of reading material than ever before. Thus, early modern readers lived in a world that had little in the way of dedicated public reading spaces, despite the profoundly public element of the marketing, procurement and consumption of text.

3.2 The Arrival of Modern Models

Modern industrial printing, newspapers, and Western-style bound books all had a transformative effect on public reading spaces in Japan. For one thing, new designs and means of production changed how books were sold. In the late Edo era, bookstores had only limited display space and most books were stored flat in piles at the back of the store. A customer walking by would check the notices with the bestsellers shown in front of the store and relay their choices to the merchant, who would then fetch the wares from inside. Bookshelves in the Western sense did not exist; in homes as well, Japanese books, having thin softcovers, could be kept in flat piles on small shelves, but were mostly put away in boxes when not in use.[77] The early Meiji era witnessed the arrival of books produced in Western styles, which, with their heavier bindings and title-bearing spines, were intended to be stored upright with the spine facing outward. Japanese bookstores adapted and by around 1900 most bookstores were configured with open shelves. They also increasingly evolved the selection process as well, moving from the older request-and-fetch model to welcoming customers to browse the shelves and make selections themselves. The typical local bookstore of the time was a one-room affair with bookshelves along the walls and traditional *hiradai* (平台) tables in the center for the dwindling stocks of books produced in the traditional format and therefore displayed flat. As Shibano Kyōko shows, the union of these two systems – and their attendant readerships, the shelves being associated with intellectual, Western works and the tables with popular, Japanese entertainment – in one space gave modern Japanese bookstores their distinct character.[78] The tables eventually came to display new arrivals or sale items, setting the foundation for the basic layout of Japanese bookstores today.

---

[77] On Edo bookstore practices, see especially Nagatomo (2002).
[78] Shibano (2008).

Meanwhile, the birth of modern mass media in the form of newspapers soon made the *yomiuri* obsolete and brought about a drastic decline in the numbers of *kashihonya*. Newspapers had better coverage than the old news-sheets hawked by *yomiuri*, carried serial fiction, the main income source for *kashihonya*, and could be read in large amounts in reading rooms for a low fee.[79] Some *kashihonya* changed their wares to newer works and kept going, a small number persisting until the end of the nineteenth century. The bulk were long since supplanted, however, by a new generation of entrepreneurs with a new type of commercial lending library. These "new-type *kashihonya*" (新式貸本屋, *shinshiki kashihonya*) were characterized by operating out of a fixed location instead of carrying their wares from house to house.[80] Some have argued that the change came about because heavy Western bindings made carrying books around impractical.[81] This is unlikely, given how traditional softcovers continued for the early years, and the most popular *kashihonya* works continued to be Edo-era fiction.[82] Neither were Western-style books for entertainment excessively heavy, even if the volumes tended to be larger. Rather, the problem was one of scale: industrial-scale publishing resulted in such a large amount of reading material that offering it from stationary locations was more practical.

Another difference between the new *kashihonya* and their Edo fore-bears was an emphasis on scholarly works and texts for students instead of entertainment and casual reading – at least at first. One of the earliest and best-known examples was Irohaya Kashihonten (いろは屋貸本店), which opened in 1885, the same year newspaper advertisements for the new *kashihonya* began to appear.[83] About 90 percent of its holdings were said to be

---

[79] Kornicki (1980), 333–334; Groemer (1994), 259–260. Newspaper reading rooms (新聞縦覧所, *shinbun jūransho*), some founded by officials and/or free of charge, spread nationwide through the 1870s but went into decline in the following decade as the cost of newspapers decreased.

[80] On "new-type *kashihonya*," see especially Asaoka and Suzuki (2010).

[81] For example, Iwasaru (2007), 155.

[82] Late Edo fiction was reprinted in moveable type and remained popular as books even as new serial literature filled newspapers and magazines.

[83] See Itō (2020a), 118. A noted account of Irohaya was Nankatei (1901–1902).

academic and the majority of its customers were students.[84] Like Irohaya, many of the new *kashihonya* were located in Kanda-Jinbōchō, a hotspot thanks to the large numbers of students there who counted on them alongside the used bookstores for affordable books.[85] Some of the new *kashihonya* had holdings that could only be read on site, some focused on books patrons could take home, and some offered a mix of services.[86]

It tends to be assumed that the new *kashihonya* were popular because public libraries were not yet commonplace.[87] This requires some qualification, however, because, as Itō Tatsuya observes, the *kashihonya* remained popular even as students, their primary users, gained increasing numbers of both school and public library options: rather than simply migrating from one institution to the other, students used both depending on their needs.[88] Part of the issue was that *kashihonya* tended to carefully curate their collections to match local users' needs, whereas the first generation of libraries were often a hodge-podge of available materials. However, libraries became increasingly important to readers, especially students, as a particular type of space, as we shall see later.

Modern schools and universities brought with them school and university libraries, as well as the first proper public libraries. It is no surprise that this era has received the lion's share of scholarly attention in library history.[89] Some of

---

[84] Kornicki (1980), 341; Iwasaru (2007), 155.

[85] For a look at *kashihonya* outside of the capital, see, for instance, Fujishima (2010) on Sapporo. A guide to starting one's own business published in 1913 included an extensive section on *kashihonya*, testifying to the impact of the industry at the time (Ishii, 1913, vol. 2, pp. 185–233).

[86] Taking a book home required paying a deposit; the amount refunded upon the book's return usually depended on for how long one kept the book (Itō, 2020a, 120). Some *kashihonya* soon developed extensive holdings of magazines and entertainment books as well.

[87] For example, Iwasaru (2007), 155. [88] Itō (2020a), 120.

[89] On the history of Japanese libraries in the context of world library history, see Tsukuda (2012) and Miura (2019). Recent landmark studies include Ogawa et al. (2016), Takayama (2016), and Shindō (2019). Library history is usually a component of library science programs in Japan, and series of texts for librarianship and information science like Minerva Shobō's (講座・図書館情報学, 11 vols.,

the credit for popularizing public libraries is usually given to prominent intellectual Fukuzawa Yukichi (福澤諭吉, 1835–1901), who mentioned them in a work based on his observations during an official mission to Europe in 1862. He stated that Western cities had libraries where people could read many books free of cost, but not take them home.[90] Shindō finds this interesting since local quasi-libraries of this nature already existed in Japan, but Fukuzawa was either unaware of this or perhaps thought little of such Japanese institutions since they were neither large nor government-run.[91] Indeed, Fukuzawa seemed to idolize the large, sophisticated, and state-managed institutions; Kornicki suggests that his mention of Westerners not being able to borrow books meant that he was probably thinking of the British Museum.[92] Modern public libraries needed to be large, state-managed, free institutions that were open to all, and if Japan had previously had libraries that fulfilled some of these criteria, it had lacked something able to meet all of them.

So it was that in 1872, prompted by an Education Ministry official's appeal, the Japanese state embarked upon a project to build a modern public library system. How this was to be done, however, was not well defined, and public libraries, like school libraries, developed in haphazard fashion. The first was likely the Shojakukan (書籍館), intended to be the library of the national museum (today's Tokyo National Museum) and modelled on the library of the British Museum. It suffered from poor management and worse finances and ended up implementing fees, moving around, and changing names until becoming the Teikoku Toshokan

2013–2019) and Jusonbō's (新・図書館学シリーズ, 12 vols., 2011–2014) include volumes on library history. Library history has been a popular field since the 1990s, and has a dedicated journal, *Toshokan Bunkashi Kenkyū* (図書館文化史研究, *Journal of the Japan Association of Library and Information History*). The JLA even has a book for students explaining how to do library history (Okuizumi, 2014). There is still little in English; Welch (1976, and its updated follow-up, 1997) provide a good overview of libraries and librarianship in Japan at the time of authorship but their historical treatments are riddled with errors.

[90] Fukuzawa (1866), 75–76. [91] Shindō (2019), 241–242. [92] Kornicki (2001), 410.

(帝国図書館, Imperial Library) in 1897 and eventually part of the National Diet Library. As Japan's first national library, its difficulties represented an inauspicious start. Nevertheless, public libraries slowly began to proliferate, and in 1892 the Japan Library Association (JLA) (日本図書館協会, Nippon Toshokan Kyōkai) was founded.[93] In 1907 it began producing *Toshokan Zasshi* (図書館雑誌, *The Library Journal*), seen as the profession's journal and still today an important library science periodical.

New institutions required new names. Initially Meiji-era libraries borrowed the term *shojakukan* from the national library, but they soon came to read the characters differently as *shosekikan*. Meanwhile, when the library attached to Tokyo Imperial University gave itself the name "図書館" (originally *zushokan*, but soon came to be read as *toshokan*), this became the go-to term for university libraries.[94] Through the late Meiji era, public libraries tended to be called *shosekikan* while university libraries were referred to as *toshokan*, with the latter word only later becoming the general term for library.[95]

The newness conferred by the names, however, was in some ways a veneer that papered over a continuity in the form of the books themselves. Some school libraries, and many public libraries, were assembled from existing *bakufu* or domain libraries, meaning the change to a modern system was often more in form than substance. With the Education Ministry having neglected to provide a clear definition of what a modern library actually entailed, some domain libraries simply rebranded themselves; in other cases local people would gather whatever books they had available, pile them in a temple storeroom or classroom, label it a library, and call it a day.[96] Some libraries were composed of whatever was bought cheap on the used book market or taken from

---

[93] It was originally Nippon Bunko Kyōkai (日本文庫協会), but changed its name in 1908.

[94] Iwasaru (2007), 151–152.

[95] Iwasaru (2007), 151–152. Note that the more traditional term for a library was *bunko* (文庫), whence derives the name of the *bunkobon* book format.

[96] For example, Shindō (2019), 260–261.

a temple in the wake of the early Meiji anti-Buddhist movement, resulting in a random assortment of reading material of negligible value to the community. Many early Meiji libraries, for all their association with "modern civilization," must have seemed, with their random collections of junk, rather poor heirs to the premodern collectors who had at least tried to preserve the knowledge of the past.[97] Moreover, most public libraries were closed-shelf through the early twentieth century, and user fees were not uncommon, making the institutions less innovative and useful than expected.

What *was* new was the use of reading space in the modern libraries, which represented a marked departure from what had come before. As new public spaces, the libraries brought with them new rules, which promptly clashed with established reading practices, none more so than noise. Enforced silence marked a significant shift, given that Edo reading spaces were just as likely to be associated with boisterous discussion as with reading quietly. Into the 1880s, it was still common to read aloud, regardless of whether the content was a magazine or a book. Maeda Ai suggested that this reading practice endured because students acquired it from studying the classics in traditional academies, while other people continued to employ it out of practical necessity since not everyone was literate.[98]

Other scholars have made similar arguments. Nagamine Shigetoshi holds that reading classical Chinese texts out loud was the dominant pattern in education and led to people routinely reading aloud even when alone.[99] Conversely, Kornicki suggests that reading aloud continued to be practiced largely in groups for sociability.[100] Reading aloud in groups certainly

---

[97] The government later only made the situation worse with the 1899 Library Law, which essentially allowed any book collection to be legally termed a library.

[98] Maeda (1973/2001), 169–170, 179–182.

[99] Nagamine (2004), 238. Reading aloud continued to be used as an instructional method for children long after silent reading had become the norm, and a generation later, seniors often saw this form of reading through a nostalgic lens (Nagamine, 1997, 72).

[100] Kornicki (2001), 268.

appears to have been more common than reading alone, but then reading in groups was itself the dominant practice.

At any rate, the phenomenon could grate on people's nerves. Foreign travelers found it particularly annoying. "When they do read, the result is worse [than the sound of playing games], for a Japanese, of whatever station, elects to read aloud in a high nasal monotone which is soul-harrowing," grumbled Irish traveler Lewis Strange Wingfield in an 1889 travelogue. "All the occupants of the twenty pigeon-holes are gabbling at once, and continue to gabble far into the night, with the confused hubbub of a Bedlam."[101] An increasing number of Japanese had come to find it annoying as well, with some complaining in newspaper letters that people should read more quietly in public spaces.[102] Reading may have frequently had a public element to it in the past, but the public would have been on a smaller scale and more likely to know the reader. Reading aloud in a modern urban setting amidst a large group of strangers represented an entirely different situation.

Consequently, modern library patrons, many of whom were used to reading aloud, had to adjust to reading silently (黙読, *mokudoku*) – or aloud but so softly as to not be heard. When combined with the undependable holdings, inconsistent organization, and procedures required to become a patron, why did readers bother? After all, as Nagamine notes, reading rooms were founded by local people and allowed reading aloud, whereas public libraries were founded by the state and imposed silent reading in top-down fashion.[103] One could add that the former also stocked material in response to the local community's needs, whereas the latter was at best unreliable on this point. As with new-type *kashihonya*, however, student users played a key role in supporting libraries. Students struggled with the rules at first, but soon came to appreciate libraries as bastions of quiet space amidst the bustling urban landscape in which conventional reading was now seen as a bother.

It was in this way that libraries became increasingly vital spaces for students. Through school life, with its frequent periods of quiet study, students began to associate silence with studying and consequently the library – the one place in the urban environment identified with silence – became configured in

---

[101] Wingfield (1889), 18–19. [102] Itō (2020a), 124. [103] Nagamine (1997), 47–51.

student culture as a study space.[104] Reading could still be done in groups, but with everyone reading quietly individually. Reading out loud was still done in groups at home for entertainment, but in libraries the group turned into a collection of individuals silently reading for study. By the turn of the century, public libraries bustled with groups of students in what had become society's default study space.

Modern libraries in Japan were thus tied to the education system, either directly (as in school libraries) or indirectly (as in public libraries expected to educate the populace but mainly serving as study spaces). With the education system and civil service both depending on exams, public libraries embraced their role as study spaces, with big tables to accommodate groups of students (Figure 12). Some institutions prepared rooms specifically for women, which came to serve as a venue for women to network.[105] Even by the end of the Meiji era in 1912, however, there were far more school libraries than public libraries in Japan, and most of the populace acquired their reading material elsewhere.[106] The Taishō era witnessed a brief increase in the number of public libraries, especially in the capital, but these struggled to recover in the wake of the 1923 earthquake and conflagration. Hibiya Library, despite being badly damaged, reopened on the day after the disaster and worked to collect and distribute information to the community, an essential commodity in the wake of the chaos.[107] Foreign countries, especially the United States, made donations and helped replenish lost collections.[108] The library model, however,

---

[104] On this point, see Nagamine (2004), 238 and Itō (2020a), 125; for an in-depth treatment of the relationship between libraries and studying, see Itō (2020b).

[105] On women's reading rooms in this era, see Aoki and Akase (2018). They show more than sixty were founded between around 1905 and 1925 (27–28).

[106] In 1911 there were 541 public libraries, of which 328 were privately operated, but most were in major centers. Yet the numbers grew: by 1941 there were 4,794, of which 1,500 were privately run (JLA International Exchange Committee [hereafter JLA], 1980, 4).

[107] Shindō (2019), 305.

[108] For instance, the Smithsonian made large donations of books ("Scientific Notes and News," 1924, 182); there were also calls for aid, such as that by a Tokyo University librarian who traveled to the United States seeking book donations ("General Announcements," 1924, 11–12).

Figure 12 Early twentieth-century libraries. Top: Okazaki City Library, 1927. Bottom: Tahara Town Library, before 1945.

remained unchanged: Mizuno Rentarō (水野錬太郎, 1868–1949), the education minister in the 1927 Tanaka Cabinet, bemoaned how Japanese public libraries were both fewer in number and much less user-friendly than their Western counterparts.[109]

Although libraries may have played only a tangential role in the reading lives of of the public, the 1920s were in many ways a golden era for reading, driven by both intellectual trends (e.g., the *Kyōyōshugi* movement) and marketing ones (e.g., the one-yen book phenomenon). Along with the emphasis on self-cultivation, the concurrent rise of popular politics, the women's movement, and labor activism emphasized the association of reading with social and political progress. This had a transformative effect on reading spaces because reading as a way of building cultural capital made the *display* of reading ever more important.

Aside from greater numbers of people reading in public – and wanting to be seen doing so – the most obvious way that this took place was with the proliferation of bookshelves throughout society. The old storage methods gave way to open, obvious shelves because whether in the home or the marketplace, books made the person, and so bookshelves became seen as a way of displaying one's character. Photographs of writers and other intellectuals at the time almost inevitably feature their bookshelves for precisely this reason.[110] The fad of publishers giving away attractive bookcases to customers was a product of the same thinking. The layout of bookstores also significantly evolved, with greater emphasis on facilitating customer browsing rather than just the convenience of the bookseller. *Hiradai* tables were set up outside to attract passersby, and while Shibano contextualizes this move as one of a number of advertising tactics employed during the one-yen boom, it is noteworthy that this practice has endured to the present.[111] Publishers, by producing works in large series meant to be

---

[109] Shindō (2019), 278–279.

[110] See, for instance, Shibano (2008), 47–48. It is telling that at a time when mass-produced furniture was only just starting to take off, bookcases were a popular item.

[111] Shibano (2008), 52–54. Bookstores were also already actively advertising in newspapers.

displayed together, and even providing specialized furniture for their offerings to bookstores, also shaped these spaces, while in addition to revamping bookstore interiors to be inviting spaces, merchants also hosted book festivals and special events.

Around this time reading groups also became much more popular, including groups that shared material for members to read (e.g. 雑誌回読会, *zasshi kaidokukai*, in which people shared magazines or pooled resources to buy subscriptions as a group), and those that read and discussed works together, transforming any available location into a social reading space. At times reading groups were organized specifically to foster education, and, especially in rural areas with less access to reading material, they served as a means of bridging the intellectual resource gap. While less numerous than their urban cousins, reading groups in rural areas played a more vital role in the community. This was unexpected: some government officials and librarians had been placing their hopes for improved rural education in public libraries. Home Ministry official (and later Tokyo governor) Inoue Tomoichi (井上友一, 1871–1919) felt that libraries needed to focus less on collecting and more on being useful to their communities; he was particularly inspired by Pittsburgh Public Library, which had been sending people to read to poor children and introduce them to the joys of reading.[112] From the turn of the century the pioneering librarian and educator Sano Tomosaburō (佐野友三郎, 1864–1920) had been at work introducing concepts like evening hours, services for children (including dedicated reading spaces), and even early mobile services at libraries he managed.[113] Yet these were exceptional cases: most communities outside major cities had to make do with poorly equipped institutions with short hours, and rural areas often had to do without.

Because villages frequently had little in the way of public reading resources aside from a simple library attached to an elementary school, or what remained of a converted *zōsho no ie*, reading groups played an even more vital role here. From the last decade of the nineteenth century, youth groups were organizing village reading groups (読書会, *dokushokai*),

[112] Inoue (1909), 105–107.

[113] On Sano, see Ogawa Tōru's biography in Ogawa et al. (2016), 24–203.

usually held at night to accommodate the locals' workday schedules.[114] Youth leaders typically would bring books or newspapers and circulate them among members to read together; there were also reading groups for local elites focused on rural development, and efforts to build small libraries.[115] By the mid-1920s, according to library scholar Iwasaru Toshio, youth group-reading activities under the loose coordination of the government were active in 96 percent of towns and villages.[116] While most coordinators no doubt had good intentions, the system later proved a convenient mechanism for a state increasingly concerned with policing public reading habits. A similar process occurred with reading programs for students that prescribed "selected books" (集団読書, *shūdan dokusho*), and indeed, by the late 1930s, the whole directed reading movement (読書指導運動, *dokusho shidō undō*) was increasingly co-opted by the state.

Serious limits on the press and freedom of speech had already been imposed with the 1925 Peace Preservation Law, intended to suppress socialists and other forces seen as a threat to the state, and the situation only deteriorated with the onset of the Second Sino-Japanese War (1937–1945) and then the Pacific War (1941–1945). Amidst heightened censorship and crackdowns, with authors and publishers punished if they were deemed problematic or insufficiently patriotic, libraries appeared a liberal indulgence and public libraries in particular entered a period of decline.[117] The Tokkō (特別高等警察, Tokubetsu Kōtō Keisatsu, or Special Higher Police), responsible for investigating "thought crimes," would sweep libraries for inappropriate material and examine patron records. The situation posed a problem for readers, especially in the urban landscape, because they had grown accustomed both to seeing reading as fundamental to modern life and to having at their disposal a plethora of reading material in the wake of the 1920s publishing boom. The decline in reading material both in terms of variety of content (given the strict censorship and preponderance of nationalistic propaganda) and in terms of the physical

---

[114] Note that *dokushokai* is also used inclusively for any kind of reading group or book club.

[115] Shindō (2019), 297–299. [116] Iwasaru (2007), 181.

[117] On the censorship regime, see Abel (2012).

experience of reading (given the poor-quality ink and paper typically employed by printers due to rationing) left the population with a rather bitter reading landscape. No wonder that children relocated from cities during wartime, as Sari Kawana shows, delighted in discovering in the countryside the colorful (both literally and figuratively) and varied books and magazines saved from a generation earlier.[118]

The authorities had been attempting to control reading practices for some time in the name of fostering national spirit, but in late 1942 the Ministry of Education dropped all pretense and issued direct instructions to the *dokushokai*, deciding both the books to be read and the nationalist ideological framework in which to do so. Instructing the public what and how to read also became a major responsibility for the public libraries as part of a broad social policy encompassing everything from schools and workplaces aimed at ensuring the citizenry read, and did so in the "proper" way.[119] The ideal of reading as the key to personal development had in essence been highjacked by the state and reorientated toward cultivating obedient subjects. However, just as some authors and publishers worked to get alternative voices past the censors, so too did some librarians quietly endeavor to undermine the official reading programs and preserve a degree of freedom within the spaces under their control.

Modernization had seen the transformation of Japanese public reading spaces through the evolution of older models and the arrival of new ones, at times interacting with each other to produce unexpected results. As we have seen, bookstores developed new ways of engaging the customer, and libraries ended up serving several social roles but not in the way initially anticipated. By the prewar period, Japan had essentially seen two distinct library trajectories come to coexist: on one hand was a collection of small, personalized, and semi-private or commercial libraries that harkened back to the early modern tradition, while on the other were the large, Western-style public libraries.[120] While the former were more local and personal, the

---

[118] Kawana (2018), 49–76. [119] See Iwasaru (2007), 227–229, and Domier (2007).
[120] The contrast between privately run local libraries and state-managed Western-style libraries is remarked upon by Shindō (2019), 360–361.

latter were more institutional and came to serve as an arm of the state. In the postwar era these would undergo further drastic transformation.

3.3 The Postwar Transformation

When the war ended with Japan's surrender in August 1945, the country's cities lay in ruins. Kanda-Jinbōchō may have gotten off relatively lightly during the systematic US bombing campaigns, but much of the capital had been devastated and large segments of the population faced unemployment, homelessness, and starvation. While the nation underwent reconstruction under the direction of the US occupation authorities and their democratization policies, the stage was set for another change in the evolution of reading spaces. Amidst the rubble, books were a valued commodity and reading retained its prewar associations with self-betterment. Now, however, the content of that process was shaped by far greater freedom for readers. With the abolishment of the Peace Preservation Law, censorship was drastically curtailed – finally ending in 1952 with the conclusion of the US occupation – and people were free to read more material than ever before. Moreover, reading represented a safe and inexpensive refuge during the struggles of reconstruction. The readership rapidly expanded among the middle and lower classes. Newspapers carried advertisements for new books on their front pages every day, and two weekly newspapers dedicated to books and publishing started in short order – practices that continue in the present.[121] Consequently, a boom occurred in public reading spaces. Libraries, bookstores, and local cafes for reading all proliferated.

Both public and school libraries expanded dramatically in the early postwar era. One reason was the occupation authorities' push for libraries as a way of establishing foundations for democracy. The association of libraries with democratic ideals was not without precedent – already in the Meiji era this potential of libraries had been recognized, which may have been one reason the ruling oligarchy was only ever lukewarm in its support for them and why the state took steps to increase its control over them from

---

[121] Namely, *Shūkan Dokushojin* (週刊読書人, *Weekly Reader*), founded in 1958 but originating from a predecessor started in 1948, and *Tosho Shinbun* (図書新聞, *Book News*), founded in 1949.

the 1920s through the war years.[122] However, the US occupation made libraries a priority and set about overhauling the library system as well as establishing a series of its own called Civil Information and Education (CIE) Libraries that served as models.[123] The CIE system – planned in September 1945, mere weeks after the occupation began, and put into effect in October – played an important role in disseminating leading research from the United States in a variety of fields (Figure 13).[124]

A key role was played by Philip O. Keeney, the US authorities' first library officer, who was largely responsible for establishing a unified Japanese public library system, one that was in many respects inspired by the success of the county library system in California.[125] The postwar libraries got off to a bumpy start, however. While in practical terms public libraries proved popular, they were less successful in fulfilling the occupation's vague mandate to fuel democracy and civics at a grassroots level.

Library scholar Takayama Masaya sees the dismissal of postwar education minister Maeda Tamon (前田多門, 1884–1962) – who was passionate about the potential of libraries to promote civics, but was purged due to his monarchism making him unpalatable to US authorities – as a missed opportunity to establish public libraries as the cornerstone of civil democracy.[126] In Takayama's assessment, public libraries became not

---

[122] As Iwasaru (2007) notes, the Freedom and People's Rights Movement (自由民権運動, Jiyū Minken Undō) in the early Meiji era supported libraries, but this was suppressed as it became increasingly politicized (164–165).

[123] On the CIE system, see Miura (2019), 241–245, and for an in-depth look, see Kon (2013). The CIE began with one library in Tokyo, but due to its popularity branches were opened in twenty-two other cities and maintained until the end of the occupation.

[124] For instance, see Suzuki et al. (2016) regarding its impact on psychology in Japan.

[125] Buckland with Takayama (2020). A lack of effective centralization and interlibrary coordination continued to plague the system in its early years. As for school libraries, see Imai (2016).

[126] Takayama (2016), 128–133. For more on Maeda and this issue, see Kumano (2007).

Figure 13 Takasaki Branch of the Tokyo CIE Library around 1949 (from the collection of Takasaki City Library).

instruments of social education as intended, but rather something akin to "free *kashihonya*" that simply offered books catering to popular demand.[127] With public libraries focusing on bestsellers rather than education, moreover, the seeds were planted for their confrontational relationship with the publishing world.[128] Professionally trained librarians were in little demand in the public system and therefore gravitated to the academic libraries and archives where they were more likely to be appreciated.[129] Yet the link between democratic ideals and the potential of public libraries was not completely stillborn; the concept persisted as an ideal, gained its fair share of defenders, and eventually took hold in popular consciousness, resulting in people beginning to associate libraries with freedom and empowerment.

Another reason libraries expanded across the spectrum was a series of important new laws. The first was the National Diet Library Law (1948) that established the National Diet Library (NDL).[130] The most important law, however, was the Library Law (1950), which required public libraries to be free, funded by taxes, and able to meet community needs. The Library Law, seen as laying the foundation for the birth of the modern public library system, eventually came to occupy an almost talismanic place in Japanese library culture, being frequently reprinted

---

[127] Takayama (2016), 132–133. The concept of postwar libraries as "free *kashihonya*" (無料貸本屋, *muryō kashihonya*) is widely used by scholars, at times as a pejorative implying libraries selling out to popular demand rather than striving to elevate their communities through education.

[128] Takayama (2016), 136. One of the long-running points of contention in postwar Japanese print culture is a reputed and occasionally bitter rivalry between publishers and bookstores on one hand and public libraries on the other, with those in the book trade accusing libraries of damaging their bottom line. Some scholars have, with justification, suggested the entire notion is silly (e.g., Itō and Uchino, 2021); also see Miyata (2013).

[129] Takayama (2016), 148–150.

[130] The NDL was based on the US Library of Congress, after the December 1947 US Library Mission arrived and made recommendations regarding administration, collection, budgeting, and so on (see "Report of the United States Library Mission," 1948; and for more on the issues (and rather paternalistic attitudes) involved, see Downs, 1949).

and celebrated by the JLA.[131] Meanwhile, the School Library Law (1953) required schools to establish libraries (although not necessarily a proper teacher–librarian to manage them). The new laws were accompanied by growing professional organizations and programs to train librarians, notably the Japan Library School (JLS), established in 1951 at Keio University.[132]

A third factor related to library expansion was increased demand. Unemployed former soldiers and munitions workers, war widows, and other demographics sought schooling and current information in order to find work, and so libraries grew in tandem with schools.[133] Unlike the prewar reading boom, this time libraries were at the center, taking on a more prominent role in daily life. Public libraries became important for three reasons: (1) convenient access to books, many of which were expensive or previously banned; (2) the need, carried over from the prewar era, to not only read but also be seen reading (and thus presumably bettering oneself); and (3) networking, especially for people rebuilding family and work lives. This established patterns that carried over to the next generation, especially as children grew up with mothers who frequented the library. Library corners or rooms specifically for children, previously unusual – Sano's pioneering efforts in the early 1900s having failed to start a trend – became much more common, and while many villages still lacked a library, they were no longer a primarily urban

---

[131] For instance, a 1980 JLA booklet on libraries spends eight of its forty-eight pages reprinting the entire law, expecting readers to intuitively grasp its significance (JLA, 1980).

[132] Before the JLS there was only a rudimentary librarian training institution established in 1921. The JLS, the first university school for library education, was founded by Robert L. Gitler with support from the American Library Association and the Rockefeller Foundation. For more, see Gitler (1999). It survives today as Keio University's Department of Library and Information Science.

[133] Libraries, like archives and research institutions, were chronically underfunded during the war years, with many unable to add to or even maintain their holdings (see, for instance, Fairbank, 1949, 9–11). Going to the library to acquire up-to-date information was thus a new phenomenon.

phenomenon.[134] Another option was bookmobiles. The first was launched in 1949, and a generation later hundreds were in operation.[135]

However, there was also another type of reading space that became immensely popular around this time, namely yet one more incarnation of *kashihonya*. This new type of *kashihonya* was once more fundamentally different from its two predecessors in several respects. First, instead of a deposit being required for each loan, the postwar *kashihonya* introduced a membership system. Roman Bunko (ろまん文庫), which opened in Kobe in 1948 and is often cited as the first postwar *kashihonya*, may have originated this system, but it was Neo Shobō (ネオ書房), a *kashihonya* chain that launched soon afterward in the same region, that proved successful enough to spread nationwide, hitting Tokyo by 1953. By then various imitators had sprung up, and it was estimated that by the mid-1950s there may have been 30,000 *kashihonya* across the country.[136] By 1957, they were a national phenomenon with an industry association and its own periodical.[137]

The second point of departure from earlier *kashihonya* was the content offered. While they started out offering novels and magazines, the primary media soon became overwhelmingly manga. Initially these were *akahon* manga, which took off first in Osaka and were named for their prewar predecessors.[138] From the early 1950s these began to be supplanted, however, by much higher-quality *kashihon* manga, which were specifically published for the *kashihonya* market by specialized publishers, many of whom got their start producing *akahon* manga.[139] Because postwar

[134] In 1959 34.3 percent of public libraries had a corner or room for children, but by 1979 this had risen to 67.5 percent (JLA, 1980, 5).

[135] See Suzuki and Ishii (1967). [136] Kajii (1976), 62–65.

[137] Kashihon Manga-shi Kenkyūkai (2006), 13.

[138] *Akahon* (赤本, red book) originally referred to books for children in the Edo era distinguished by red covers; in the Meiji era it became a general term for cheap, disposable fiction aimed at young people and hawked from street stalls. *Akahon* manga were small booklets where the paper, printing, and often artwork, were of poor quality.

[139] See Kashihon Manga-shi Kenkyūkai (2006) for a thorough look at *kashihon* manga. On the history of manga in general, see Shimizu (1991) and Sawamura (2020), and in English see Johnson-Woods (2010).

kashihonya were first and foremost about manga, they were not in direct competition with libraries and therefore thrived alongside them just as their Meiji predecessors had. As the modern manga industry dramatically expanded through the 1950s, *kashihonya* remained the dominant way to access manga, but this was not the only reason for their popularity. *Kashihonya* served as the primary public reading space for children (Figure 14), and the social experience of reading manga at the local *kashihonya* with one's friends after school features in many memoirs of those who grew up in the early postwar era.[140]

Some *kashihonya* began to incorporate elements of cafes, coming to resemble reading cafes with refreshments. There were also cafes that catered to readers with books and magazines, although given how prevalent reading was at the time virtually any cafe or restaurant served as a reading space: a decade later in the late 1960s, reading remained the nation's most favored pastime.[141] Whereas in the prewar era bookstores and cafes enjoyed – despite being used by a wide variety of readers – a reputation as elite, intellectual social spaces, the postwar conception was more inclusive. In addition to focusing on manga and other popular reading material, the early postwar *kashihonya* and reading cafes endured despite public libraries increasing in number and holdings because the former adopted a more explicitly local focus and were often more conveniently located than public libraries in most urban neighborhoods. The appeal of enjoying reading with friends over drinks and conversation also gave them an edge as social spaces over the still rather sterile, quiet environment of the public libraries.

Yet even when it came to public libraries, it was routine to visit with friends and family. This was because amidst these changing reading spaces, in the 1950s much reading, especially entertainment reading, continued to take the form of shared reading, a practice that likely persisted for economic as well as social factors. When family members or friends pooled their

---

[140] There are also memoirs specifically about *kashihonya*, including Kikuchi (2008) and Hasegawa (2018). For an analysis of *kashihonya* against the social backdrop of the era, see Takano (2016).

[141] A 1968 survey of leisure activities put reading first, ahead of travel, film, watching sports, and other pastimes (Uemura, 1969, 174).

Figure 14 Children at a *kashihonya*, circa 1956.

resources they could easily buy more books or magazines to enjoy together as a group than if they had sought to acquire them individually. It is no surprise that the same practice then carried over into public spaces, where, whether in a boisterous cafe or a quiet library, people enjoyed reading together as a shared activity. In an era when families still tended to be quite large and individuals enjoyed less private space, going somewhere to read with relations or friends was an attractive proposition. Students would go to read together after school, while workers would follow a similar pattern after work, often visiting cafes or small restaurants where they could read over noodles or drinks.

Another important reading space was trains and train stations. Reading on the train had developed early on and already become commonplace by the early 1920s.[142] Publisher Iwanami Shigeo, mentioned in the previous chapter, specifically wanted red *shinshobon* covers that would stand out on the train.[143] In the postwar era, however, trains became one of the most common public reading spaces due to the expanding rail network and the large number of daily commuters from the suburbs. Commuters became recognized as a distinct readership, and selling books and magazines to them in station kiosks became widespread.[144] *Bunkobon* and *shinshobon*, being pocket-sized, were perfectly suited for this purpose: as Uchiyama Saeko observes, from the late 1950s in popular conception trains had become "places to read books" and *shinshobon* "books you take to read on the train."[145] Trains and train stations also became sites for the exchange of reading material, with people leaving magazines for other commuters to pick up, a phenomenon that endured even into the 1990s.

In the mid-1960s, as public libraries continued growing, they experienced something of a change in public perception. Various libraries and associations sought to encourage awareness of the value of libraries to communities. The JLA in particular seized on the association of libraries with democracy the occupation authorities had encouraged, and began to actively foster the idea of libraries as bastions of civic consciousness, freedom, and empowerment, helping root the image more firmly in popular consciousness. In 1963, the JLA released a report (中小都市における公共図書館の運営, "Management of Public Libraries in Small and Medium-sized Cities") that set out proposals for library staffing, acquisitions, management, and funding, but called for a focus on users rather than administrative matters, and did so in language emphasizing the role of libraries in serving and ensuring the intellectual freedom of their communities.[146] The report and a follow-up 1970 book (市民の図書館,

---

[142] On the development of reading on trains, see Nagamine (2004), 81–113.

[143] Yoshino (1964), 137–138. [144] Uchiyama (2005), 161.

[145] Uchiyama (2005), 161–162.

[146] JLA (1963); often referred to as "中小レポート."

Citizens' Libraries) were influential texts used as policy guides for local libraries in drawing up services for their communities.[147]

The JLA also kicked its Library Law fetishization into high gear, declaring April 30 (the day the law was passed in 1950) national Library Day in 1971. This helped make sure that as libraries became more strongly associated with democracy in public consciousness, the Library Law was a central motif. Against the backdrop of rising activism and democratic consciousness in the late 1960s (in Japan as elsewhere), there was a push for the liberalization of access to education and knowledge, and this cemented the link between libraries and democracy, which also came to be reflected in pop culture (as shall be seen later).[148]

The emphasis on serving the community, coupled with a new generation of young librarians better trained and more receptive to local needs than their predecessors, brought about practical innovations such as better services for children. *Kodomo bunko* (子ども文庫, children's libraries) and the similar *katei bunko* (家庭文庫, home libraries), informal private libraries people established in their homes as reading spaces for neighborhood children, had existed in various forms since the turn of the century, but were inadequate for the expanding postwar population, prompting parents to demand more of the public library system. This resulted in more branch libraries and an improved focus on offering material for children in a welcoming reading space.[149] In rural areas, some libraries instituted systems where books were circulated to families through children attending school. Circulation, however, remained a minor role for both public and school libraries. While the public made extensive use of reference services and came to count more on public libraries as a community information resource, they saw libraries as first and foremost spaces *to go and read*: like *kashihonya* and other institutions since the Meiji era, a library was a place to

---

[147] JLA (1970).

[148] Works reflecting on libraries in Japan, especially those by librarians, thus also consider their role from perspectives informed by democracy, civil society, and public empowerment (e.g., Shimada, 2019).

[149] Such informal children's libraries, often just called *bunko*, still exist and are usually run by volunteer mothers. For an overview, see Robles (2009).

read or study and borrowing books was not a major concern. Ignorant of this history and baffled by low circulation figures in spite of the large number of library visitors in Japan, George Chandler (later the director-general of the National Library of Australia) wondered in 1971 (apparently in all seriousness) whether one factor was that "traditional Japanese pastimes like the tea ceremony and flower arrangement took up much time which might otherwise be devoted to reading."[150] While the idea of the library as primarily a reading space for its community, rather than a place from which to borrow books to read at home, struck him as bizarre, this had remained the general view among many readers.

This did not mean that those spaces remained static; in fact, far from it. The 1960s and 1970s witnessed a significant shift in reading practices brought on by socioeconomic changes. Urbanization increased tremendously, nuclear families became far more common, and personal income increased substantially.[151] Education became more affordable. Schools expanded greatly, and so did libraries and bookstores.[152] Not only were more books readily available than ever before, but it was also far easier to buy them. There were also far more magazines, including large regular manga magazines that began in the 1960s, some of which by the 1970s enjoyed circulations of more than a million. With greater varieties of reading material readily available in bookstores and libraries, the way they were enjoyed also changed. Building a personal library became a common practice among members of many middle-class families, and as these books became personal possessions their enjoyment became a more private affair. Usually such changes are explained in terms of wealth: with higher income and greater spending power, more people could afford to buy commodities, including books, for themselves.

---

[150] Chandler (1971), 149.

[151] In 1950, 53 percent of the population was urban (United Nations, 2019, 35) and this skyrocketed over the next two decades. For specific statistics on Japanese socioeconomic development, see Miwa and Hara (2010).

[152] Take universities, for example: in 1945 there were only around 50, whereas by 1970 there were nearly 400. Today there are almost 800 (MEXT, 2020).

However, this was only part of the answer because another factor was how urbanization and changes in family life brought about transformations in the use of space. With intensifying urbanization, more and more families were renting or purchasing residences in the large cities. Whereas families were more likely to have large residences in the countryside, they usually needed to share these with grandparents, uncles and aunts, and siblings. In the cities, by contrast, although they were living in much smaller residences amidst high population density, like *danchi* apartments (perhaps comparable to Soviet *Khrushchyovka*), they also felt a greater ownership of those spaces, as urban families shifted to the nuclear model. Such residences were seen favorably as a hallmark of convenient modern living, while also coming in for criticism due to the values of consumerism and privacy – and thus a departure from the traditional sense of community – with which they were associated.[153] The move to smaller residences encouraged a shift toward social spaces that were smaller and more personalized than before. Compared to previous generations, the experience of space in Japanese cities became more individualized or compartmentalized.

It was in this context that reading practices changed again, as social reading largely gave way to private reading. Reading predominantly at home became much more common, although public reading spaces remained popular. The latter responded by reorganizing their spatial delineation, gradually creating smaller, more intimate divisions of space. Bookstores, usually such spaces already, did not see much of a change in layout, although one could argue there was perhaps less tolerance for people standing around reading for long periods. In libraries, as readers spent more time reading at home, circulation finally jumped dramatically, a development aided by open stacks becoming the norm and trained librarians having a firmer grasp on what their communities wanted to read.[154] The layout in libraries varied depending upon the location, given how this involved a complex interaction among library administration and the community of users, but a general trend saw urban libraries adopting more individualized space than did rural libraries.

[153] Neitzel (2016). [154] See, for instance, Nagata (2007), 3–4.

Compartmentalizing space made sense given how library architecture tended to resemble a set of boxes.[155] Whereas before major libraries often had large reading rooms with seating for hundreds, newer libraries incorporated subdivisions or a series of smaller rooms. The large, open tables that had previously dominated libraries became fewer in number, while smaller individual study spaces, which had remained limited, expanded. This trend continued through the 1980s and onward, as semi-separate desks, and rows of carrel desks, already common in school libraries, came to occupy more space in public libraries as well. Putting a chair at the end of each stack was one effort to make the most "individual space" out of a shared environment. By the 2000s, some libraries had almost cubicle-like divisions for readers, while the limited multimedia areas of the 1990s evolved into a series of private desks or booths where patrons could listen to audiobooks or watch DVDs with headphones. Essentially, as reading became less social and more private, library space became gradually tailored more for individuals and less for groups.

While this shift in space usage might be termed a "shrinking," it occurred as public libraries were increasing in number, and increasing available reading space, while at the same time promoting an "open" approach (per JLA efforts like the aforementioned 1970 book) to the community to make libraries more welcoming. Moreover, as this change advanced over the years, some library activities based on the older social reading model – such as reading sessions for children – gradually became less frequent.[156] Library cutbacks in the wake of the economic downturn in the 1990s began to deprive some libraries of professional staff and proper budgets, which also hurt such activities.

The change was most obvious, however, with the manga cafes (漫画喫茶, *manga kissa*), that came to fill the void left by the *kashihonya* that had all but disappeared by the late 1960s. While there may have been earlier forebears, and cafes with reading material available were by no means new, it is generally agreed upon that manga cafes evolved out of coffee shops in the late 1970s, most

---

[155] On the evolution of Japanese library architecture, see Igarashi and Lee (2021).

[156] More open reading spaces for children, and attendant activities, persisted long after those for adults had been increasingly compartmentalized.

prominently an establishment called The Magazine (ザ・マガジン) in Nagoya that hit upon the idea of charging a flat hourly rate for access to an extensive manga collection, with refreshments requiring additional payment.[157] Their standard clientele were the legions of male office workers, but groups of students were common, and on the weekends, mainly in smaller towns, one might see families come by.

The manga cafes had more spatial demarcation than their predecessors of a generation earlier, and this increased as time wore on through the 1990s. From the mid-1990s, manga cafes began introducing internet-capable computers and transforming into or being replaced by newly established net cafes (ネットカフェ, *netto kafe*), with still smaller spaces and a computer per desk, now clearly set off from the manga stacks in the corridor.[158] In contrast to the *kashihonya* with their hordes of children or the colorful social spaces of the early manga cafes, the net cafes, many of which were chains, evolved into dark spaces with rows of tiny cubicle rooms. They thus represent an extreme example of miniature self-spaces within a broader public space.

By the mid-2000s, some of the homeless population was essentially living in them, a group the media dubbed "net cafe refugees." Many net cafes still exist, but despite their sizeable manga collections it remains utterly inconceivable for groups of children or families to visit one for a group reading session. The compartmentalization of many reading spaces seems somewhat ironic given how Japanese business culture by and large rejected 1990s US-style cubicles in favor of retaining open offices. Recent years, however, have seen a range of responses to the changing character of public reading spaces, engendering yet a further stage of transformation.

[157] A Nagoya city guidebook from 1982 described The Magazine as possessing 30,000 volumes, with coffee and cake costing 400 yen to start and 200 yen for each additional hour (Our City Corporation, 1982).

[158] Some net cafes still call themselves manga cafes, and "pure" manga-only cafes still exist, a number of which utilize a certain theme to appeal to a clientele of fans.

3.4 Contemporary Trends: Looking Back, Looking Forward

Changes in reading practices occurring against a backdrop of socioeconomic transformation and the ongoing digital revolution associated with ubiquitous smartphone use are frequently seen as heralding a decline in reading and thus the end of public reading spaces. News reports of a drop in youth reading and libraries closing in small towns appear to confirm this. The actual situation, however, is more complex. The same surveys that indicated youth were reading less indicated that this was not correlated with smartphone use.[159] Rather, it seems that the students who read the most were also more likely to be the heaviest users of smartphones. Nevertheless, with ebooks, visual novels, and other aspects of the virtual reading world – the topic of the next chapter – established, surely public reading is a thing of the past, and hence the library closures? Yet this too is not what it appears to be due to the emptying of the Japanese countryside now that nearly 92 percent of the population is urban.[160] Library closures have been limited, occurring in towns suffering from severe depopulation rather than lack of use per se. These are not vibrant towns ignoring their libraries, but rather dying towns where businesses and public services have been closing as the remaining population drops to nil. In some cases, village and town mergers have led to library collections being consolidated. Populated, active towns, on the other hand, also have well-attended libraries.

Public libraries remain important spaces for their communities. Seniors depend on the libraries as a social space, often gathering in study rooms to read together, chat, and have tea until the student rush arrives on school afternoons. Student groups use libraries less than in the past, but this is also because cafes with books and, conversely, bookstore cafes, are now also welcome places for students to study together. Extending library hours into the evening also boosted circulation. Libraries, like many public spaces, closed or limited access in 2020 during the coronavirus pandemic, which presented a significant problem for their communities, and as restrictions were eased they started filling with patrons again. The overall trend since at least the mid-1990s has seen an increase in public library holdings, numbers

---

[159] The primary survey being the annual NFUCA one (NFUCA, 2021).
[160] United Nations (2019), 37.

of books borrowed, and the number of library-card holders – as well as the old grumbling from publishers who continue to blame library success for hurting book sales (Figure 15).[161]

Japan's public reading spaces have continued to transform in response to changing reading practices and the needs of their communities. The lines between establishments are also becoming somewhat blurred, as some chain bookstores have been morphing into reading cafes, while some libraries have followed suit – not without controversy. In 2003, changes to the law enabled public library management to be outsourced to the private sector, leading to some libraries being overhauled with new services and cafe spaces to attract visitors.[162] In particular, a media furor ignited when the Tsutaya bookstore chain took over the Takeo City Library, with the new multimedia options and cafe services attacked by social critics but conversely embraced by many patrons. Some of the controversy concerned the merging of libraries and cafes, but this was hardly a new phenomenon.[163]

A more serious issue was the role of private corporations in public libraries, recalling the complex relationship between *kashihonya* and libraries since the Meiji era.[164] Information science scholar Ōtani Takushi, taking stock of the criticism of "Tsutaya libraries," identifies a key issue as the creation of a cultured space for people who do not usually use libraries, while observing that libraries have evolved historically and in an era with a plethora of reading options the role of libraries would naturally continue to change.[165] Mizunuma Yuhiro and Tsuji Keita found that, contrary to assumptions, outsourced libraries often performed better than public ones,

[161] "Popularity of Japanese Libraries Hitting Publishers' Bottom Line" (2018).

[162] See Fukumoto et al. (2017).

[163] Some public libraries had coffee bars in the 1970s, and it was not unusual for postwar library branches to occupy community centers with adjacent cafes and performance spaces. Kawamoto and Tsuji (2018) showed that, as of 2015, more than half of public libraries and nearly two-thirds of university libraries allowed food and drink.

[164] Sometimes this was more subtle, such as the "sponsor system" (スポンサー制度) through which a business pays for a library's magazines and receives recognition in return.

[165] Ōtani (2016); for further analysis, see Satō (2016).

Public Library Collections, Book Loans, and Registered Users

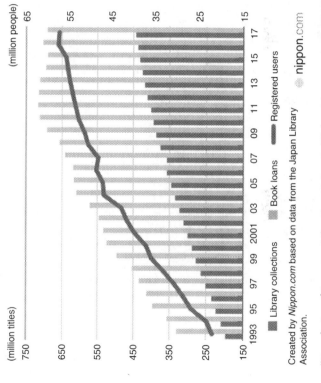

Created by *Nippon.com* based on data from the Japan Library Association.

Figure 15 From "Popularity of Japanese Libraries Hitting Publishers' Bottom Line" (2018) (Nippon.com).

possibly because they were more likely to hire trained librarians with the skills to improve library services.[166] The importance of librarianship is evident, while the fact that people were sensitive to changes in libraries demonstrates how seriously communities value these spaces.

In the case of libraries, however, the majority that remain under direct public management have also undergone changes to incorporate various activities and create an open, inviting space – producing what some architectural scholars have dubbed a "complex library."[167] While this tends to be seen as a new direction, it could conversely be understood as arising from embracing libraries' long history as functional reading spaces and thereby seeking to craft a comfortable environment conducive to reading activities. This is interesting in light of a trend observed since the early 2000s of people reading less at home, but going outside to read more frequently.[168] There has thus been a virtuous circle of people going to the library to enjoy reading in a pleasant environment and libraries working to create comfortable reading spaces. Newly constructed facilities often take this into consideration, such as the Gifu Media Cosmos (opened in 2015, and incorporating Gifu City Chūō Library, an activity space, and exhibition galleries) and the Nakanoshima Children's Book Forest (built in Osaka's Kita Ward in 2020 by the architect Andō Tadao, who donated the library to the city so children could have access to a wide range of books in a comfortable space). Meanwhile, hotels and resorts have introduced or expanded reading spaces, and there are temporary library installations, such as the Autumn Foliage Library (紅葉図書館, Kōyō Toshokan) in Karuizawa, Nagano Prefecture that is set up in a park with refreshments for several weeks each autumn (Figure 16).

Several factors underlie this rethinking of public reading spaces. One is simply increased wealth enabling people to buy more books than before, while from the early 2000s the used book market has only expanded, with Book Off, an enormous chain of used bookstores, making books extremely

---

[166] Mizunuma and Tsuji (2019).

[167] For example, Kawashima and Murosaki (2019). Also see Igarashi and Lee (2021) on evolving library architecture in light of current trends.

[168] See, for instance, Sukigara and Taniguchi (2002).

cheap and easily accessible. Then there is the gradual rise of ebooks, and the impact of Amazon and online retailing, which were slow to start in Japan, but have continued to rise – developments only exacerbated by the coronavirus pandemic. The upshot of all this has been that the role of libraries and booksellers in just providing books has become less significant, prompting a focus on not the books themselves, but on offering a pleasant environment in which to encounter and enjoy those books. This dovetails with a recognition of reading spaces as therapeutic spaces: thus, spaces with books that are also conducive to comfortable reading are attractive. As in other countries, people tend to like living near libraries and bookstores, not only for convenience but because reading spaces are seen as attractive and nourishing settings in which to raise a family.[169] It is not surprising that the impact of public reading spaces on their surrounding social environment, and their role in connecting communities together, continues to attract attention.[170]

Numerous book-related events also play a role. One of the most interesting is Bibliobattle (ビブリオバトル), a library event originating at Kyoto University in 2007 that soon led to other universities and then national competitions. Participants have five minutes in which to introduce a book to the audience, like a rapid-fire book review session, with the best presentation declared the winner.[171] A particularly significant trend is an effort to bring back various forms of social reading. There are many reading groups, and these are growing. Unlike book clubs in North America, modern Japanese ones normally meet in cafes rather than homes and may incorporate group reading as well as discussion, in some ways echoing the older reading practices discussed earlier.[172] Reading groups are popular

---

[169] Real estate agencies tout proximity to reading spaces as a selling point. For instance, the January 2022 Saitama Prefecture issue of Suumo's free information magazine for renters had a cover story entitled "Ten Libraries That Are the Pride of Their Localities" (*Suumo Shinchiku Manshon*, 2022).

[170] For example, Igaya (2014).

[171] For the official Bibliobattle webpage, see www.bibliobattle.jp.

[172] For an analysis of contemporary reading groups, see, for instance, Yorioka and Hoshino (2020).

Figure 16 Reading corner at Hot Spring Resort Matsunoi (Minakami, Gunma Prefecture, December 2020).

enough that there are even books explaining their benefits and how to join or start one.[173] Some libraries, schools, or whole towns encourage forms of group reading (共同読書, *kyōdō dokusho*): Noshiro City (Akita Prefecture), for instance, declared every third Sunday "Family Reading Day."[174] There is also "morning reading" (朝の読書, *asa no dokusho*), where students and teachers have a free reading period in class, and "family reading" (家読, *uchidoku*), where families read together and discuss their impressions. While these movements, gaining popularity since the mid-2000s, tend to be considered innovations, they are essentially various forms of older reading practices resurrected by people who miss the social benefits. The microlibrary trend – small private libraries managed by individuals or groups – has also been recognized for connecting people, and like the children's libraries harkens back to the tradition of small private libraries in Japan in contrast to the state-managed ones.[175]

How have booksellers responded to recent trends in reading practices? One approach has been to expand their offerings to a wider variety of media. Book Off sells used video games and manga alongside books and advertises a multimedia approach, in that customers can buy the novel, comic, and game adaption of a popular franchise all in one location. Other chain bookstores sometimes carry home decor, while independent bookstores may offer handicrafts, artwork like photography, and other things alongside books. Both new and used bookstores face pressure from Amazon, which intensified during the coronavirus pandemic from 2020 when online book purchases soared. Some booksellers opt to sell books on Amazon Marketplace or run their own websites for online retailing. Many used bookstores sell items through Nihon no Furuhonya (日本の古本屋, kosho.op.jp), an online retail website managed by the Tokyo Association of Dealers in Old Books (東京都古書籍商業協同組合, Tōkyōto Koshoseki Shōgyō Kyōdō Kumiai) that has some 900 affiliated booksellers.

---

[173] For example, Yamamoto (2019).
[174] See the official page at www.city.noshiro.lg.jp/section/kyoiku/gakushu-sports/shogai-gakushu/10332.
[175] See Shindō (2019), 361–366.

Many bookstores have worked to create bright, inviting spaces and have like libraries increasingly renewed their focus on the experience of reading.[176] Some have incorporated cafes, mirroring the process begun with *kashihonya* and manga cafes much earlier. While one trend just mentioned was booksellers augmenting their holdings with non-book wares, conversely another trend is specialized book offerings: bookstores specialize in business books, books related to anime, and the *bunko* book format, all running alongside the older specialty bookstores like the Mandarake (まんだらけ) chain that sells used manga and collectibles. There are also innovative practices like "secret book" (秘密の本, *himitsu no hon*), where the customer buys a covered book recommended by the bookseller.[177] Cities and travel websites have taken note of the culture of pleasure reading and book collecting, leading to more and more articles and travel plans pertaining to local bookstores.[178]

In a similar vein to the awareness of book spaces as therapeutic spaces, another contemporary trend has been merging books with other experiences. One approach brings together various bookstores and other shops to make a nice place for bookish people to shop, such as Hankyū Kosho no Machi (阪急古書のまち), an antiquarian book street in Osaka's Kita Ward that in 2017 was reconstituted next to a new bookstore and other stores and was well received. Some stores focus on being attractive reading spots, like Tsutaya Daikanyama, which comprises several buildings offering all manner of works and a cafe, and which earned a spot on Flavorwire's "The 20 Most Beautiful Bookstores in the World."[179] The real innovation often comes from independent booksellers and cafe owners, however, such as combining books with certain refreshments (e.g., Book and Beer in Kitazawa, Tokyo), classy retro reading cafes (e.g., Akihabara Nagomidō, inspired by the Taishō era), or inns with libraries so guests can read all night

---

[176] See Hon no Zasshi Zenshūbu (2018) for examples of contemporary bookstore designs.

[177] One example of such a bookseller is Fukuro Shosabō (梟書茶房, Owl Book Cafe) in Ikebukuro, Tokyo. The author has also encountered secret book vending machines.

[178] For just one example, see Travel Note (2017). [179] Temple (2012).

long (e.g., Book and Bed in Ikebukuro, where bunk beds adjoin bookshelves). There are also reading tours and reading retreat spaces, such as Books and Retreat in Yugawara, Kanagawa Prefecture (Figure 17). The important thread binding all these ventures is not books per se but rather the community of readers and the joy of reading.

There is, of course, also the fan market to consider: the plethora of *dōjinshi* (同人誌, indie or fan comics) events where amateur manga artists sell their work to fans, the most famous such event being Comic Market, or Comiket (コミケット), held twice a year at Tokyo Big Sight.[180] Likely the largest fan event in the world, it is a special space where fan fiction meets bookselling.

3.5 Reflections on Transforming Public Reading Spaces

The history of public reading spaces in Japan is one of both expansion and evolution, as spaces bound to certain ideals and practices of reading transformed over time. In many ways it is also a story of the interaction between private and state-run institutions, with the specific makeup and role of those actors in public reading lives changing with each generation. This can be seen through three different forms of *kashihonya* and in the evolution of public libraries from study spaces to community resources and finally locales for comfortable reading. Some public reading spaces came into existence to serve a specific reading community's needs, and in turn transformed when those needs changed. The interconnected history of reading practices also demonstrates a cyclic character, such as how social reading among family and friends experienced a decline but has now gone through a resurgence. It could be that, in a world ever more mediated by virtual forces, the search for authenticity has led to a renewed interest in the real-time experience of exploring literary worlds with others.

---

[180] On *dōjinshi*, see Noppe (2014).

Figure 17 Books and Retreat, March 2022.

4 Virtual Reading Spaces

This brings us to the last type of reading space to consider in modern Japan, that which exists in the virtual realm. What I mean by "virtual" here encompasses two distinct senses: first, the imaginary, covering the representation of reading spaces, as in pop culture; and second, the digital, including both virtual spaces for discussing or otherwise engaging with conventional reading, and new modes of reading. The shift to increasingly private reading discussed in the previous chapter was itself enhanced by new reading experiences that came about through technological innovation. While the need for brevity prevents anything more comprehensive than scratching the surface, the chapter will touch on a variety of different media and trends that comprise the reading world of contemporary Japan.

4.1 Problematizing Reading in Contemporary Japan

Analyzing changing patterns of reading requires an awareness of not only genre but also media, as evolving forms of literary media engender new reading opportunities. Contrary to expectation, new forms do not always replace their predecessors, but just as often stand alongside or even reinforce them through broad cultural complexes. A vast amount of manga, for example, draws directly or indirectly on classical and modern literature: there is a plethora of manga adaptations of Heian romances, medieval tales, and early modern warrior epics, and Japanese authors themselves appear as characters in the fictional worlds of no small number of manga, television dramas, and games. Along with media mixes and pop culture franchises, the cultural complexes mediating past and present literature to craft new reading experiences are beginning to attract scholarly attention.[181]

---

[181] On media mix (メディアミックス), akin to transmedia storytelling, see Steinberg (2012). The narratives, characters, and other creative elements of mixes and franchises as a form of media content are called *contents* (コンテンツ), giving rise to *contents tourism* (コンテンツツーリズム) and related terms. On the contents industry, see Kabashima (2009). On manga adaptations of classical literature see, for instance, Ivanova (2021) in an issue of *Japanese Language and Literature* dedicated to such adaptations.

One of the most interesting recent developments, which took shape in the 1990s but has come to the forefront since the 2000s, has been light novels (ライトノベル, *raito noberu*), a form of young adult fiction that evolved from the intersection of popular entertainment fiction and manga thematics and style. Major genres are fantasy, science fiction, and romance, and tones range from maudlin to tongue-in-cheek parody aimed at genre-savvy youth. While prose works, they are heavy on dialogue and feature manga-style illustrations, as well as an inclination toward long and/or silly attention-catching titles – for example, *That Time I Got Reincarnated As a Slime* (転生したらスライムだった件, 2013–2015) or *Do You Love Your Mom and Her Two-Hit Multi-target Attacks?* (通常攻撃が全体攻撃で二回攻撃のお母さんは好きですか?, 2017–2020).[182] Light novels are extremely popular and have taken their place alongside manga as the origin of numerous multimedia franchises.[183]

As new media have led to new reading experiences, blanket statements about a decline of reading, especially among youth – touched upon in the previous chapter – become increasingly problematic. Surveys asking how much time people devote to reading usually employ the term *dokusho* (読書), which on one hand literally means "reading books," but for many people connotes time spent with a paper volume in hand – not the primary method of reading for many young people, who enjoy ebooks and light novels via smartphones or tablets.[184] Such readers may consume

---

[182] Many works mentioned in this chapter have official translated titles; thus, the English renderings are put before the Japanese.

[183] Light novels remain smaller than the enormous manga industry, but numerous series have sold tens of millions of copies. The first light novel series to launch a franchise was likely *Slayers* (スレイヤーズ) in the 1990s, while the 2010s saw *Sword Art Online* (ソードアート・オンライン) and *Re:Zero – Starting Life in Another World* (Re:ゼロから始める異世界生活), both of which began as online novels, trigger enormous transmedia franchises once they became light novels. For more on light novels, see Ichiyanagi and Kume (2013) and Ōhashi and Yamanaka (2015–2016).

[184] Some commentators have pointed out this problem, noting the decline in "reading" has been accompanied by a large increase in people reporting enjoying ebooks and so on (e.g., Kaya, 2020).

large amounts of reading material, but are unlikely to respond in the affirmative when asked if they enjoy *dokusho*. There is also an element of moral panic: historically, every innovation in media has given rise to new reading practices that prompt concern over people not reading, or not reading the "right things," whether that be vernacular fiction, foreign works, manga, or now ebooks. This is hardly limited to Japan.[185] However, the changing reading landscape does reinforce the importance of critical and comparative approaches to readership.[186]

4.2 Representing Reading Spaces

Alongside literary adaptations, and works orientated around reading and all manner of readers – such as the light novel and manga series *Book Girl* (文学少女, 2006–2013) and *Bibliophile Princess* (虫かぶり姫, 2016–present) – there is no shortage of portrayals of reading spaces in the Japanese pop culture sphere. The preponderance of depictions of physical reading spaces speaks to their significance in society, but at the same time is almost always idealized or romanticized in nature rather than realistic. In the case of libraries, fantasy novels, manga, and games overflow with depictions of incredible, magical libraries, often inspired by the libraries of early modern European noble houses, while modern Japanese school and public libraries feature as sites of humor, intrigue and youthful romance.[187]

---

[185] See, for instance, Ross (2018) on similar moral panics regarding reading in North America.

[186] For instance, on the practices involved in girl readerships encountering and responding to fictional portrayals of girls, see Aoyama and Hartley (2011) and Berndt et al. (2019); on manga literacy, see Ingulsrud and Allen (2009); and on *otaku* culture, see Galbraith et al. (2015).

[187] Manga examples include fantasy works like *Magus of the Library* (図書館の大魔術師, 2017–present), a celebration of the magic of reading, or *The Farthest Library beyond the Mirror* (鏡のむこうの最果て図書館, 2019–2020), about a library at the end of the world, and real-world works like *The Library at Dawn* (夜明けの図書館, 2010–2020), about a reference desk librarian, or *Master of the Library* (図書館の主, 2011–2017), about a librarian at a children's library. Light novel examples include *Tokimeki [Heartbeat] Library* (トキメキ図書館, 2012–2018), a children's series about a girl who loves books making friends in

Yet even modern libraries are seldom depicted in a realistic manner: large, long tables and cramped stacks echo an earlier era because invoking the space associated with established genre tropes – studying with one's first crush in the school library, getting help with an assignment from a librarian, discovering a mysterious hidden book – is more important than depicting libraries as they currently look. The need to convey to the audience "This is a library!" through stereotypical imagery – even in science fiction, where archives resemble stacks but with data banks rather than books, even if this arrangement would make no sense to a machine – leads to reviewers inevitably commenting that the reading spaces are not realistic, but ultimately this comes down to libraries persisting in pop culture as symbols of imagination, freedom, and romance. It is what libraries represent, more than what they look like in reality, that most informs these depictions.

These concerns spill over into how librarians are depicted as well – not as the detached stereotypical figures I recall from many US films, but as active knowledge workers. Libraries serving as a source of knowledge is a common theme in much Western literature, but in modern Japan they are more strongly and directly associated with empowerment, fueled by prewar associations between reading and status ala *Kyōyōshugi*, and postwar thinking that reading meant freedom and social progress. There is a real historical underpinning behind the depictions of librarians solving mysteries and helping people with their problems, but in fantasy settings this is taken to the extreme, with librarians often appearing as great sages or sorceresses. The characters of Meteora in the *Re:Creators* (レクリエイターズ, 2017) anime and Patchouli Knowledge from the *Touhou Project* (東方Project) games (Figure 18) are wise and powerful figures in their respective universes, wielding magical power derived from long years of study, while the

a new town, *Let's Go to the Library on a Sunny Day* (晴れた日は図書館へいこう, 2013, 2020) about a girl solving mysteries with the help of her librarian cousin (based on a 2003 children's book), *Karakusa Library Visitor's Registry* (からくさ図書館来客簿, 2013–2016), a fantasy work about a library in Kyoto that attracts odd visitors, and *Yoyo and Umi's Library Date* (世々と海くんの図書館デート, 2020–present), a twist on the library romance trope that follows a fox-girl who falls in love with a boy at the library.

Figure 18 *Patchouli Knowledge* (パチュリー・ノーレッジ) from the *Touhou Project* games by Team Shanghai Alice (fan illustration by krs [www.pixiv.net/artworks/94238340]).

Re:Zero franchise features the spirit librarian Beatrice. Meanwhile, Victorique in the *Gosick* (ゴシック, 2003–2011) light novel series, set in an alternate 1920s Europe, is neither a librarian nor a magician but spends all her time in the library and uses her genius to solve crimes.[188]

The consistent theme in these fictional representations is libraries as a source of power and agency, especially for women, ranging from the awkward but genius schoolgirl to the sorceress.

---

[188] Another interesting case is Index from the *A Certain Magical Index* (とある魔術の禁書目録, 2004–2010) light novels (and subsequent franchise), who has been mentally imprinted with a collection of banned books and is thus essentially a living library.

The association of libraries with freedom and democracy, on the other hand, a notion discussed in the previous chapter, takes its most over-the-top form in *Library Wars* (図書館戦争), a franchise about local communities forming paramilitary organizations to protect their libraries from an oppressive government bent on censorship and control (Figure 19). Perhaps only in Japan would people taking up arms to fight and die for their library be a viable storyline!

Of course, the strong association between libraries and freedom in the popular consciousness means that from an audience perspective, if there were to be a "last stand" of democracy, it would occur at the libraries, which speaks to how communities value their libraries and what they stand for.

Whereas libraries are associated with the abstract ideals of knowledge and freedom, bookstores in pop culture are associated more with folksy wisdom and local romance. Bookstore owners and clerks are frequently depicted as playing important roles in their local communities, providing advice or getting caught up in their customers' lives whereupon humorous hijinks inevitably ensue (Figure 20).[189] Some of these depictions, like *Booking!!* and *Skull-face Bookseller Honda-san* convey real aspects of managing a bookstore, while others are entirely romanticized. As was the case

[189] For instance, the manga series *Akari of the Forest Bookshop* (本屋の森のあかり, 2006–2013), a romance about bookstore clerks, and *Kingyo Used Books* (金魚屋古書店, 2000–2020), about a used bookstore specializing in old manga that inspires its customers, or the novel *I Learned Everything Important about My Work from a Little Bookstore in Amagasaki* (仕事で大切なことはすべて尼崎の小さな本屋で学んだ, 2020), where a new employee at a publisher gains insights from the owner of a small bookstore. Other examples include manga series *The Electric Town's Bookstore* (デンキ街の本屋さん, 2011–2017), *The Story of the Little Wife in the Bookstore in That Shopping Street* (あの商店街の、本屋の、小さな奥さんのお話。, 2013–2015), *Skull-face Bookseller Honda-san* (ガイコツ書店員本田さん, 2015–2019), *Booking!!* (ぶっきんぐ!!, 2017–2018), and the light novel and then manga series *Biblia Used Bookstore Casebook* (ビブリア古書堂の事件手帖, 2011–present). *Biblia* saw a television adaptation in 2013, while in 2015 a television drama called *Fight! Bookstore Girl* (戦う!書店ガール) about two women working in a bookstore was popular.

Figure 19 Advertising for the live-action *Library Wars* film (2013).
(Provided by TBS)

Figure 20 Examples of manga and light novels revolving around bookstores.

with libraries there have also been various fantasy works about bookstores – such as Natsukawa Sōsuke's (夏川草介, 1978–) whimsical novel *The Cat Who Saved Books* (本を守ろうとする猫の話, 2017) about a teenage boy who inherits his grandfather's used bookstore and goes on a quest with a talking cat to save books from people who have mistreated them – and even *kashihonya*.[190]

It should come as no surprise that Kanda-Jinbōchō also features in popular culture depictions, such as in the 2003 film *Café Lumière* (珈琲時光), in which romance blooms between a bookstore clerk and a cafe worker in the town, or the manga and anime series *Dropkick on My Devil!* (邪神ちゃんドロップキック, 2012–present), in which the protagonist lives in the town and buys magical tomes there.[191] Comiket also has its fair share of appearances, such as when the cast of the *Lucky Star* (らき☆すた, 2003–present) franchise visit.

4.3 Digital Reading Spaces

The digital transformation of everyday life engendered by the spread of the Internet was initially comparatively slow to take off in Japan, given the low numbers of households with personal computers in the 1990s, but exploded with the spread of smartphones in the late 2000s. This, in turn, brought about various new reading experiences mediated by the digital realm. These

---

[190] Natsukawa's work is now a bestseller in English translation. Other examples include the manga series *Welcome To My Book Store in Another World!* (異世界の本屋さんへようこそ!, 2016), the light novel and then manga series *The Haunted Bookstore: Gateway to a Parallel Universe* (わが家は幽世の貸本屋さん, lit. *Our House Is a Haunted Kashihonya*, 2019–present), and historical romantic light novels like *The Kashihonya and Occasional Love-Letter Store* (貸本屋ときどき恋文屋, 2016), set in the Edo period, or *A Thousand and One Nights in London* (倫敦千夜一夜物語, 2015), about a *kashihonya* in Victorian England (!).

[191] The anime also features a song about poor student life in Kanda-Jinbōchō, which proved popular enough to be crowdfunded and recorded in an extended version. There have also been pop culture characters named after the town, such as Jinbō in Kihara Toshie's manga *Nue* (鵺), part of her Dream Monuments (夢の碑, 1984–1997) series.

come in many flavors, the first and most immediate of which is simply the act of reading online.

One of the earliest and most influential examples of an online reading resource was Aozora Bunko (青空文庫, lit. "blue sky library," but fig. "open air library"), which drew on works out of copyright and evolved as a Japanese equivalent to Project Gutenberg. Overall, however, Japan was a relative latecomer to the ebook world, especially when it came to contemporary works. Japanese public libraries possess only a fraction of the digital resources of their US counterparts, although some have been enthusiastic about putting local materials and rare works online, and the National Diet Library and prefectural libraries have been leaders in this area.[192]

Why was this the case? One reason was access: demand for books, magazines and manga in digital format only took off when smartphones did, and these remain how the bulk of the Japanese population engages with the digital world. Sociocultural factors were also involved: the aging population meant that seniors' tastes were more heavily represented, and there remains in contemporary culture an enduring love of physical media – print books, music CDs, DVDs, and so forth. Another reason was publishers, which were unenthusiastic about digital reading options. Small-scale publishers lacked the resources to enter the digital marketplace, while larger ones were reluctantly dragged along by consumer demand, gradually making magazines and manga, and to a lesser extent books, available online.[193] While the absolute numbers remain low, from 2010 to 2020 digitization of manga more than doubled, that of novels and light novels doubled, and that of practical/how-to works more than tripled.[194]

---

[192] On ebooks and digital libraries, see Yamazaki et al. (2012). For the NDL's digital collection see https://dl.ndl.go.jp.

[193] Both the publishing world and the government were partly motivated by a desire to fend off manga piracy, both domestically and internationally, by offering legal alternatives.

[194] Takano and Hori (2021), 6. Some publishers offer classic works with high-quality scans of the original prints alongside optical character recognition (OCR) renderings of the text.

The coronavirus pandemic intensified this development considerably: the publisher Kōdansha announced in February 2021 that its digital content sales had surpassed that of their paper content for the first time.[195] Websites like DMM.com and DLsite offer large amounts of digital manga, *dōjinshi*, and games; Amazon offers ever-increasing ebook and manga offerings for its Kindle platform, and major publishers also provide options specifically tailored for mobile users. Consequently, trains remain public reading spaces, with most commuters counting on their smartphones.

Alongside providing a new platform for print media, the digital world has also engendered new forms of reading. Some proved to be fads that did not long endure, such as phone novels (ケータイ小説, *keitai shōsetsu*): short, catchy works, often written by young women and designed to be read on flip-phone screens. These were a phenomenon in the mid-2000s, with some popular enough to be republished as paper books that became bestsellers, but they were largely derided and disappeared when smartphones and tablets made it possible to read conventional full-size novels on the go. More successful over the long term were, and are, online novels (オンライン小説, *onrain shōsetsu* or ネット小説, *netto shōsetsu*), a digital renewal of serial fiction that flourishes across websites like Let's Read Novels! (小説を読もう!, yomou.syosetu.com), Become a Novelist (小説家になろう, syosetu.com), and novelist.jp. Like their counterparts in other digital spheres around the world, Japanese online novels can be written and read by anyone. They are carefully followed by editors from major publishing houses, which may offer popular authors a deal to rewrite their work as a light novel or manga series, occasionally triggering an influential franchise, as was the case with the aforementioned *Re:Zero*. There are, naturally, copious amounts of fan fiction to be found as well, and while fans continue to focus on print *dōjinshi*, digital versions thereof as well as other forms of fanfiction have certainly found a home in the virtual realm.

---

[195] "Denshi + Kenri ga 'Kami' Uwamawaru" (2021). Kōdansha's income from paper books and magazines was down 1.2 percent, whereas its digital income was up 19.4 percent.

Then there is the digital gaming world, which has its own history of reading experiences, a topic increasingly attracting scholarly attention.[196] In Japan there are games that are based on books or about books (such as *Genji Monogatari*), and of course games that within their own synthetic worlds contain books that can be read by players to bring the world to life. A particularly noteworthy reading experience, however, is the visual novel (ビジュアルノベル, *bijuaru noberu*), a type of interactive fiction that combines text with art and audio (music, sound effects, and voices).[197] First developed in the early 1990s, in the 2000s visual novels experienced a boom across not only the personal computer game market – which they came to dominate – but also the more popular and lucrative console and portable game system markets.[198] In terms of mechanics, visual novels normally consist of a large text box on the bottom of the screen that conveys narration and dialogue while the top half of the screen portrays a background image with character images in the foreground, depicted with changing expressions or outfits as appropriate.[199] For particularly important scenes, these may be replaced by a unique image (called CG, "computer graphics"), momentarily filling the whole screen. Because the player–reader moves the multimedia story along at their own pace (and can often save their progress), even simple visual novels constitute what electronic literature scholar Espen Aarseth called "ergodic literature."[200]

---

[196] See, for instance, the 2019(1) issue of *Publije, e-revue de critique littéraire* dedicated to reading and gaming.

[197] While the status of visual novels as "games" is a matter of contention among Anglophone gamers, in Japan this is not an issue; moreover, visual novel sequences feature in many other types of games as a means of moving along plot or character development.

[198] Chunsoft's 1992 *St. John's Wort* (弟切草) is often considered the progenitor of the modern visual novel format. For background, see Kabashima (2009).

[199] This combination of text, image, and sound evokes *kamishibai* (紙芝居, paper theater), a type of visual storytelling popular from the 1930s until the early postwar era, when it declined in the face of manga magazines and television anime. See Nash (2009).

[200] Aarseth defined "ergodic literature" as literature where "nontrivial effort is required to allow the reader to traverse the text" (1999, 7). Some visual novels

Degree of player–reader influence over the narrative itself ranges from none (so-called kinetic novels) to extensive, where a large number of branching plot paths and endings are possible.[201]

Visual novels often borrow the aesthetics and thematics of manga and light novels, but some are more literary and may draw on classical literary styles and tropes. They are comparable to light novels in that they tend to be heavily dialogue driven, but are frequently more focused on characters rather than exciting plots, and it is thus no surprise that one of the most popular genres is romance. There are also, however, great numbers of fantasy and horror works, and those that aspire to be thoughtful or melancholy – some visual novel studios take pride in crafting emotional rollercoasters, nick-named *nakige* (泣きゲー, lit. "crying games") by fans.[202] Particularly popular visual novels launched not only sequels but anime adaptations or whole pop culture franchises, examples being the courtroom puzzle-solving *Ace Attorney* (逆転裁判, lit. "turnabout trial," 2001), long fantasy epic *Fate/stay night* (2004), and science-fiction *ChäoS;HEAd* (2008, first entry in the Science Adventure series). Influential developers include Key, whose tear-jerkers *Kanon* (1999) and *CLANNAD* (2004) also became anime hits; Nitroplus, famous for eerie works like *Song of Saya* (沙耶の唄, 2003) that merges Lovecraftian horror with warped sexuality; Type Moon, known for the aforementioned Fate series; and Chunsoft, whose *428: Shibuya Scramble* (428〜封鎖された渋谷で〜, 2008) enjoyed tremendous critical success.[203] Because of their nature, visual novels have also served as a means to subvert

could be compared to "choose your own adventure" books or hypertext works in terms of their basic mechanics, but many transcend these to create immersive and emotional reading experiences that have proven influential across popular culture.

[201] "Kinetic novel" was adapted from KineticNovel (キネティックノベル), a brand of visual novel by Visual Arts. At the other end of the spectrum are the works of Key, infamous for labyrinthian plot paths.

[202] Note that thematic categories like *nakige* are, like fantasy or romance, not limited to visual novels.

[203] Other influential visual novels include *Utawarerumono* (うたわれるもの), the Danganronpa (ダンガンロンパ) series, and *Umineko: When They Cry* (うみねこのなく頃に).

tropes, play with narrative formulations, and offer commentary on the meaning of reading and the relationship between reader and text.[204] The format has since gone global with visual novels produced and enjoyed around the world in many dedicated communities.[205]

As is the case elsewhere, the Japanese internet is a vibrant reading landscape in which reading clubs and forums, social media platforms like Twitter, and dedicated smartphone apps like ReadHub connect readers in the virtual realm. Social media has fanned the flames of fandom for new works as well as drawn attention to older ones: several of the biggest bestsellers in 2021 were originally published years earlier, such as Shigematsu Kiyoshi's (重松清, 1963–) *Vitamin F* (ビタミンF, 2001), but exploded on social media as readers exchanged recommendations during the coronavirus pandemic.[206] Books recommended by TikTok content creators enjoyed skyrocketing demand – prompting publishers and booksellers alike to take notice – and despite the recommendations being virtual, most of the resulting purchases were of print books.[207]

Another significant development, occurring in parallel with the renewed interest in group/social reading touched on at the end of the previous chapter, has been an increase in online reading groups. Essentially the phenomenon is a return to the old *dokushokai* model, but conducted in virtual space, and often with people one only knows online – though the echoes of the past are missed by contemporary commentators who often see social reading as a new phenomenon. Nevertheless, the value of social reading through virtual mediation – whether for understanding,

[204] Works by Nitroplus are particularly known for this, notably *You and Me and Her: A Love Story* (君と彼女と彼女の恋。, 2013). In the Anglosphere, the American *Doki Doki Literature Club!* (2017) enjoyed success as a horror deconstruction of romance visual novel tropes and the relationship between player–reader and in-game character, but this was already well-trodden ground in the Japanese visual novel scene.

[205] The Visual Novel Database (https://vndb.org) lists an enormous number of professional and amateur works, and is growing exponentially. As of March 2020, it listed 27,000, and as of June 2021, more than 30,000.

[206] See, for instance, Shinchōsha (2021).

[207] See "TikTok de Shojaku wo Shōkai = Bakuhatsuteki Hitto" (2021).

Figure 21 VTuber Fumi (フミ, R), with her guest fellow VTuber Amemori Sayo (雨森小夜, L), go through viewer responses to Murata Sayaka (村田沙耶香)'s novel *Convenience Store Woman* (コンビニ人間, 2016), May 2020 (https://www.youtube.com/watch?v=0hYkI1q14lk)

collaborative study, or just socialization – has been recognized by both journalists and scholars.[208] Naturally, Twitter is replete with hashtags for people seeking to connect with others to discuss books.[209] The coronavirus pandemic fueled not only the growth of all these trends but also real-time virtual reading events. While author readings and book reveals going virtual was to be expected, there have also been growing numbers of virtual *dokushokai* (バーチャル読書会) where people read together and discuss books via Zoom or other meeting platforms. Virtual YouTubers (VTubers) like Fumi cover books with their fans (Figure 21), while social games and

---

[208] See, for example, Takei (2012), Hashimoto (2014), and Matsumura and Nunokawa (2020).

[209] For example, #本好きな人と繋がりたい ("want to connect with people who love books"), #読書好きな人と繋がりたい ("want to connect with people who love reading").

virtual reality (VR) platforms like VRChat have seen their own virtual *dokushokai*: just the newest version of something already encountered several years prior, with players assembling their colorful and eccentric avatars not to go hunt dragons, but to read to each other and discuss their favorite books. In some senses we have truly come full circle.

4.4 Reflecting on Virtual Reading Spaces

Representation of reading spaces tends to be idealized or follow traditional tropes, even though, as seen in the previous chapter, change is ongoing; simultaneously, the digital world has witnessed many innovations, including new ways to experience and engage others about reading. It is still too early, I believe, to truly trace the impact of virtual reading communities, consisting of complex networks of readers not only discussing works but engaging in creative responses, crafting their own fiction, and commenting on the work of others. This, of course, is a global phenomenon, where we can witness new forms of public reading space – public not in a geospatial sense, but in the community sense. In the case of Japan, many of these readers fly under the radar – online books and light novels are not always considered books, one "plays" rather than "reads" a visual novel in Japanese, and readers crafting their own spaces in the virtual world do not show up in statistics. Nevertheless, new readers and new reading experiences, and the ways that they build on what came before, deserve our attention.

5 Conclusion

As reading practices have transformed over time, so too have reading spaces, shaped by economic change, social upheaval, technological innovation, and disasters. When the coronavirus pandemic hit in early 2020, while no lockdown was imposed in Japan, most libraries and booksellers temporarily closed due to states of emergency and there was a concern – just as had been the case following everything from the Great Kantō Earthquake to the arrival of digitization – that this would be the end of reading spaces and print culture altogether. While some booksellers did ultimately go out of business, for the most part the panic was overblown. Rather than reflecting a lack of demand, the rapidly aging population meant that many older business owners took the pandemic as an opportunity to retire, a phenomenon by no means limited to the book trade.

While there was a big blow to print culture, it was not books, but magazines, that suffered, with around a hundred print magazines folding by some estimates. As with store closures, however, this was already a developing trend before the pandemic: magazines, always an extremely competitive market in modern Japan, were the part of print culture that was the first, and most successful, to go digital, with magazines either moving online or being supplanted by new digital alternatives. Reading, however, shot up during the pandemic, including among young adults: for while print publishing continued a slow decline – although in the manga sector this was offset by the phenomenal success of the *Demon Slayer* (鬼滅の刃) series – digital sales continued to climb, accounting for nearly a quarter of publications for 2020.[210]

The problem for many readers, with libraries and bookstores closed, was where to find material, which drove more people online seeking used books and digital options. Many publishers provided free online offerings, while online book retailers, including Amazon, were even in March 2020 overwhelmed by demand. The e-hon service – managed by distributor Tohan

---

[210] This was even picked up by the English-language media in Japan; see "'Demon Slayer' helps Japan print sales see smallest drop since 2006" (2021) or "Japanese young adults reading more than before pandemic" (2020).

Corporation and enabling customers to buy from their preferred bookstore – flourished. More small-scale publishers began direct online retailing to customers and many more used bookstores commenced online selling.

Bookstores also responded to the pandemic in innovative ways, such as holding online events or scaled-down in-person events open to limited numbers of customers. A number of small or hobbyist bookstores also appeared in local communities; some, like Kame Books – a side project by a bookseller in Ichikawa, Chiba Prefecture, so small that only one person could enter at a time – enjoyed media attention.[211] Major reading events like the Kanda Book Fair and Comiket were cancelled in 2020 for the first time in their histories, but Comiket was back in late 2021 and the Kanda Book Fair in spring 2022, both well attended. As libraries began to reopen, they too held events and exhibitions, and there have been book events in department stores and elsewhere.

This book has been an attempt to briefly trace how various forms of reading space in modern Japan, from book towns and public reading spaces to the virtual world, have transformed over time. This has not been a simple leap from a "traditional" to a "modern" model – however appealing such reductions may appear – but a multifaceted and ongoing process. As reading moved from an activity with a strong social component to a quiet, private pursuit, only to have its social and environmental aspects rediscovered by a more recent generation, reading spaces continually evolved to suit readers' changing needs. Many localities have themselves embraced books and reading alongside Kanda-Jinbōchō, such as Misato (Saitama Prefecture), which markets itself as "Japan's #1 Reading Town" (日本一の読書のまち). New media and new communities have diversified reading experiences, while libraries, booksellers, and the virtual landscape have in different ways rekindled social reading by recapturing and celebrating the experience of reading and not just books per se. The only certainty going forward is that as readers and reading continue to evolve and diversify, so too will subsequent generations of reading spaces.

---

[211] "Nihon-ichi Chiisai kamoshirenai Honya" (2020).

References

*All Japanese works published in Tokyo unless otherwise indicated.

Aarseth, E. J. (1999). *Cybertext: Perspectives on Ergodic Literature*. Baltimore, MD: Johns Hopkins University Press.

Abe, Y. (1957). *Iwanami Shigeo-den*. Iwanami Shoten.

Abel, J. (2012). *Redacted: The Archives of Censorship in Transwar Japan*. Berkeley: University of California Press.

Agnew, J. A. (1987). *Place and Politics: The Geographical Mediation of State and Society*. Winchester, MA: Allen and Unwin.

Akiyama, Y. (2002). *Meiji no Jānariʐumu Seishin: Bakumatsu, Meiji no Shinbun Jijō*. Gogatsu Shobō.

Amano, I. (2009). *Daigaku no Tanjō*. 2 vols. Chūō Kōronsha.

Amano, I. (2016). *Shinsei-Daigaku no Tanjō*. 2 vols. Nagoya: Nagoya Daigaku Shuppankai.

Aoki, R. and Akase, M. (2018). "Meiji/Taishō/Shōwa senzenki no fuetsuranshitsu." *Toshokan Bunkashi Kenkyū* 35, 21–51.

Aoyama, T. and Hartley, B. (2011). *Girl Reading Girl in Japan*. London: Routledge.

Asaoka, K. and Suzuki, S., eds. (2010). *Meiji-ki "Shinshiki-Kashihonya" Mokuroku no Kenkyū*. Sakuhinsha.

Beach, S. (1959). *Shakespeare and Company*. New York: Harcourt, Brace and Company.

Berndt, J., Nagaike, K., and Ogi, M., eds. (2019). *Shōjo across Media: Exploring "Girl" Practices in Contemporary Japan*. Cham: Palgrave Macmillan.

Berry, M. E. (2007). *Japan in Print: Information and Nation in the Early Modern Period*. Berkeley: University of California Press.

Buckland, M. with Takayama, M. (2020). *Ideology and Libraries: California, Diplomacy, and Occupied Japan, 1945–1952*. Lanham, MD: Rowman and Littlefield.

Chandler, G. (1971). *Libraries in the East: An International and Comparative Study*. London: Seminar Press.

Checkland, O. (2003). "Maruzen and the foreign book trade." In *Japan and Britain after 1859: Creating Cultural Bridges*. New York: Routledge, pp. 59–72.

Clements, R. (2015). *A Cultural History of Translation in Early Modern Japan*. Cambridge: Cambridge University Press.

Covatta, A. (2017). "Density and intimacy in public space: A case study of Jimbocho, Tokyo's book town." *Journal of Urban Design and Mental Health* 3(5). www.urbandesignmentalhealth.com/journal-3-jimbocho.html.

"'Demon Slayer' helps Japan print sales see smallest drop since 2006." *Kyodo News*. January 25. https://bit.ly/3GalB30.

"Denshi + kenri ga 'kami' uwamawaru." (2021). *Sankei News*. February 19. http://sankei.com/economy/news/210219/ecn2102190018-n1.html.

Domier, S. (2007). "From reading guidance to thought control: Wartime Japanese libraries." *Library Trends* 55(3), 551–569.

Downs, R. B. (1949). "Japan's new national library." *College and Research Libraries* 10(4), 381–387, 416.

Fairbank, W. (1949). "News of the profession." *Far Eastern Quarterly* 8(4), 451–467.

Fitch, N. R. (1983). *Sylvia Beach and the Lost Generation: A History of Literary Paris in the Twenties and Thirties*. New York: Norton.

Frank, J. (2017). *Regenerating Regional Culture: A Study of the International Book Town Movement*. London: Palgrave Macmillan.

Frederick, S. (2006). *Turning Pages: Reading and Writing Women's Magazines in Interwar Japan*. Honolulu: University of Hawai'i Press.

Fujishima, T. (2010). *Kashihonya Dokuritsusha to sono Keifu*. Sapporo: Hokkaidō Shuppan-kikaku Sentā.

Fukumoto, N., Shiwa, F. and Nakano, Y. (2017). "Raikan mokuteki to taizai kūkan kara mita fukugō kōritsu toshokan no riyō jittai." *Nihon Kenchikugakkai Kyūshū-shibu Kenkyū Hōkokushū* 56, 65–68.

Fukuzawa, Y. (1866). *Seiyō Jijō.* Vol. 1. Shōkodō. https://iiif.lib.keio.ac.jp/FKZ/F7-A0201/pdf/F7-A02-01.pdf.

Galbraith, P. W., Kam, T. H. and Kamm, B., eds. (2015). *Debating Otaku in Contemporary Japan: Historical Perspectives and New Horizons.* London: Bloomsbury.

"General announcements" (1924). *Bulletin of the American Association of University Professors* 10(3), 4–12.

Gitler, R. (1999). *Robert Gitler and the Japan Library School: An Autobiographical Narrative.* Ed. M. Buckland. Lanham, MD: Scarecrow Press.

Groemer, G. (1994). "Singing the news: Yomiuri in Japan during the Edo and Meiji periods." *Harvard Journal of Asiatic Studies* 54(1), 233–261.

Hasegawa, Y. (2018). *Kashihonya no Boku wa Manga ni Muchū datta.* Sōshisha.

Hashimoto, M. (1964). *Nihon Shuppan Hanbaishi.* Kōdansha.

Hashimoto, Y. (2014). "Shūgōchu de yomu rekishi shiryō: Smart-GS ga jitsugensuru gurūpu rīdingu." *Jinbun Jōhōgaku Geppō* 37. www.dhii.jp/DHM/DHM37_smartgs.

Hioki, K. (2009). "Japanese printed books of the Edo period (1603–1867): History and characteristics of block-printed books." *Journal of the Institute of Conservation* 32(1), 79–101.

Hon no Zasshi Henshūbu, ed. (2018). *Nippon no Honya.* Hon no Zasshisha.

Huffman, J. L. (1997). *Creating a Public: People and Press in Meiji Japan.* Honolulu: University of Hawaii Press.

Ichita. (2018). "Hon wo yomanai wakamonotachi: Netto wa saikyō na no ka? Hon wo naze yomubeki na no ka wo kangaeru." *Ichita no Matsuri Nisshi* blog. May 5. https://creative-ict.net/archives/755.

Ichiyanagi, H. and Kume, Y. (2013). *Raito Noberu Sutadīzu.* Seikyūsha.

Igarashi, T. and Lee, M., eds. (2021). *Nihon no Toshokan Kenchiku: Kenchiku kara Purojekuto e*. Bensei Shuppan.

Igaya, C. (2014). *Tsunagaru Toshokan: Komyuniti no Kaku wo Meʒasu Kokoromi*. Chikuma Shinsho.

Imai, F. (2016). *Nihon Senryōki no Gakkō Toshokan: Amerika Gakkō Toshokan Dōnyū no Rekishi*. Bensei Shuppan.

Ingulsrud, J. E. and Allen, K. (2009). *Reading Japan Cool: Patterns of Manga Literacy and Discourse*. Lanham, MD: Lexington Books.

Inoue, Takaaki (1981). *Kinsei Shorin Hanmoto Sōran* (Nihon Shoshigaku Taikei, vol. 14). Musashi Murayama: Seishōdō Shoten.

Inoue, Tomoichi (1909). *Jichi Yōgi*. Hakubunkan.

Ishii, K. (1913–1914). *Dokuritsu Jiei Eigyō Kaishi Annai*. 7 vols. Hakubunkan.

Ishizuka, J. (1998). "Enpon wo henshūshita hitobito: Kaizōsha-ban gendai Nihon bungaku zenshū to gendai." *Shuppan Kenkyū* 29, 29–48.

Itō, K. and Uchino, Y. (2021). *Honya to Toshokan no Aida ni arumono*. Yūkensha.

Itō, T. (1994). *Shuppan Ōkoku Kōdansha*. Ōesu Shuppansha.

Itō, T. (2020a). "Dokusho sōchi toshite no kashihonya to toshokan." *Yamaguchi Kokubun* 43, 117–130.

Itō, T. (2020b). *Kugaku to Risshin to Toshokan: Paburikku Raiburarī to Kindai Nihon*. Seikyūsha.

Ivanova, G. (2021). "Reading the literary canon through manga in the twenty-first century." *Japanese Language and Literature* 55(1), 163–179.

Iwanami, Shigeo. (1927). "Dokushi ni yoseru: Iwanami Bunko hakkan ni taishite." Iwanami Shoten.

Iwanami, Shoten, ed. (1996). *Iwanami Shoten Hachijū-nen*. Iwanami Shoten.

Iwasaru, T. (2007). *Nihon Toshokanshi Gaisetsu*. Nichigai Associates.

"Japanese young adults reading more than before pandemic" (2020). *Japan Times*. October 26. www.japantimes.co.jp/news/2020/10/26/national/japanese-young-adults-reading-coronavirus.

Jinbōchō ga Suki da! (2019). "Ika ni Shite 'Hon no Machi' wa Dekita no ka" special issue. www.books-sanseido.co.jp/jimbocho/pdf/Jinbocho_sukida_13.pdf.

"Jinbōchō, Tokyo" (2020). *Wikipedia*. October 21.

Japan Library Association (JLA) (1963). *Chūshō Toshi ni okeru Kōkyō Toshokan no Unei*. Japan Library Association.

Japan Library Association (JLA) (1970). *Shimin no Toshokan.* Japan Library Association.

Japan Library Association (JLA) International Exchange Committee (1980). *Libraries in Japan*. New ed. Japan Library Association.

Johnson, A. (2018). *Book Towns: Forty-Five Paradises of the Printed Word*. London: Frances Lincoln.

Johnson-Woods, T., ed. (2010). *Manga: An Anthology of Global and Cultural Perspectives*. New York: Continuum International.

Kabashima, E. (2009). "Kojin seisaku kontentsu no kōryū to kontentsu sangyō no shinka riron." *Tōkyō Daigaku Daigakuin Jōhōgakkan Kiyō: Jōhōgaku Kenkyū* 77, 17–41.

Kageyama, M., Tomatsu, M. and Iyama, N., comps. (1849–1862). *Edo Kirie-zu*. National Diet Library Collection.

Kajii, J. (1976). *Sengo no Kashihon Bunka*. Tōkōsha.

KANDA Renaissance Shuppanbu, ed. (1996). *Kanda Machinami Enkaku Zushū*. Kubokōmuten.

Kashihon Manga-shi Kenkyūkai, ed. (2006). *Kashihon Manga Returns*. Popurasha.

Kashima, S. (2017). *Kanda-Jinbōchō Shoshi-machi Kō: Sekai Isan-teki "Hon no Machi" no Tanjō kara Genzai made*. Chikuma Shobō.

Kato, N. (2022). *Kaleidoscope: The Uchiyama Bookstore and its Sino-Japanese Visionaries*. Hong Kong: Earnshaw Books Ltd.

Kawamoto, M. and Tsuji, K. (2018). "Toshokan-nai inshoku-kahi ni kansuru jittai-chōsha." *Library and Information Science* 79, 85–107.

Kawana, S. (2018). *The Uses of Literature in Modern Japan: Histories and Cultures of the Book*. London: Bloomsbury Academic.

Kawashima, S. and Murosaki, C. (2019). "Taizaigata fukugō toshokan ga riyō kōdō ni ataeru kōka ni kansuru kenkyū." *Nihon Kenchiku Gakkai Taikai Gakujitsu Kōen Kōgaishū* 2019, 97–98.

Kaya, K. (2020). "'Wakamono no Hon-banare' wo nageku shuppan gyōkai no ōki na machigai." *JBPress*. January 27. https://jbpress.ismedia.jp/articles/-/59093.

Keaveney, C. T. (2009). *Beyond Brushtalk: Sino-Japanese Literary Exchange in the Interwar Period*. Hong Kong: Hong Kong University Press.

Kikuchi, A. (2012). "Higashi Nihon daishinsai to shuppan gyōkai: Mizō no jitai ni dō taiōshita no ka." *Shuppan Kenkyū* 43, 119–131.

Kikuchi, M. (2008). *Bokura no Jidai ni wa Kashihonya ga atta: Sengo Taishū-shōsetsu Kō*. Shinjinbutsu Ōuraisha.

Kobayashi, F. (1991). "Kinsei kōki ni okeru 'zōsho no ie' no shakaiteki kinō ni tsuite." *Rekishi* 76, 25–43.

Kon, M. (2013). "CIE infomēshon sentā no katsdō." In M. Kon and M. Takayama, eds., *Gendai Nihon no Toshokan Kōsō: Sengo Kaikaku to sono Tenkai*. Bensei Shuppan, pp. 87–154.

Kōno, K. (2013). *Monogatari: Iwanami Shoten Hyakunen-shi, vol. 1: "Kyōyō" no Tanjō*. Iwanami Shoten.

Konta, Y. (1977/2009). *Edo no Honya-san: Kinsei Bunkashi no Sokumen*. Heibonsha.

Kornicki, P. F. (1980). "The publisher's go-between: *Kashihonya* in the Meiji period." *Modern Asian Studies* 14(2), 331–344.

Kornicki, P. F. (2001). *The Book in Japan: A Cultural History from the Beginnings to the Nineteenth Century*. Honolulu: University of Hawaii Press.

Kudō, K. (2011). "Kinsei chiiki shakai ni okeru zōsho to wan ani ka: Chiiki 'chi' no shiryōron-teki kenkyū wo mezashite." *Kokubungaku Kenkyū Shiryōkan Kiyō: Ākaibusu Kenkyū-hen* 7, 35–60.

Kumano, R. (2007). "The US occupation and Japan's new democracy." *Educational Perspectives* 40(1), 36–43.

Kurita, K., ed. (1968). *Shuppanjin no Ibun: Kōdansha: Noma Seiji.* Kurita Shoten.

Lee, L. O. (1999). *Shanghai Modern: The Flowering of a New Urban Culture in China, 1930–1945.* Cambridge, MA: Harvard University Press.

Mack, E. (2010). *Manufacturing Modern Japanese Literature: Publishing, Prizes, and the Ascription of Literary Value.* Durham, NC: Duke University Press.

Maeda, A. (1973/2001). "Ondoku kara mokudoku: Kindai dokusha no seiritsu." *Kindai Dokusha no Seiritsu.* Iwanami Shoten, pp. 166–210.

Maeda, T. (2018). *Edo no Dokushokai: Kaidoku no Shisōshi.* Heibonsha.

Marshall, A. B. (2019). *Magazines and the Making of Mass Culture in Japan.* Toronto: University of Toronto Press.

Maruzen Kabushiki-gaisha, ed. (1980). *Maruzen Hyakunenshi: Nihon Kindaika no Ayumi to tomo ni.* Maruzen.

Matsuki, S. (1986). *Honya Ichidaiki: Kyōto Nishikawa Seikōdō.* Chikuma Shobō.

Matsumura, K. and Nunokawa, H. (2020). "Sōsharu rīdingu ni oite tasha no rebuy ga dokusho ni motarasu kōka." *Nihon Kansei Kōgakkai Ronbunshi* 19(3), 269–273.

Meech-Pekarik, J. (1986). *The World of the Meiji Print: Impressions of a New Civilization.* New York: Weatherhill, 1986.

MEXT. (2020). "Monbu Kagaku tsūkei yōran." www.mext.go.jp/b_menu/toukei/002/002b/1417059_00006.htm.

Miura, T., ed. (2019). *Tosho/Toshokanshi: Toshokan Hatten no Kishikata kara Mietekurumono.* Kyoto: Minerva Shobō.

Miwa, R. and Hara, A., eds. (2010). *Kingendai Nihon Keizaishi Yōran.* Tōkyō Daigaku Shuppankai.

Miyata, N. (2013). *Toshokan ni Kayō.* Misuzu Shobō.

Mizunuma, Y. and Tsuji, K. (2019). "Investigation of public libraries managed by outsourcing: A study focusing on library usage, opening days, and directors' librarian qualifications and workloads." *IIAI International Journal of Service and Knowledge Management* 3(2), 62–81.

Moretti, L. (2020). *Pleasure in Profit: Popular Prose in Seventeenth-Century Japan.* New York: Columbia University Press.

Moroi, T., and Takemura, M. (2004). "Kantō jishin (1923/9/1) ni yoru higai yōin-betsu shishasū no suitei." *Nihon Jishin Kōgakkai Ronbunshū* 4 (4), 21–45.

Nagamine, S. (1997). *Zasshi to Dokusha no Kindai.* Nihon Editāsukūru Shuppanbu.

Nagamine, S. (2004). *"Dokusho Kokumin" no Tanjō: Meiji Sanjū-nendai no Katsuji Media to Dokusho Bunka.* Nihon Editāsukūru Shuppanbu.

Nagata, H. (2007). "Public libraries in Japan: Triggers for the renovation of library service models." [Paper presentation]. Congresso Internacional: La Biblioteca Publica, Medellin Colombia. www.kc.tsukuba.ac.jp/div-comm/pdf/Library_in_Japan.pdf.

Nagatomo, C. (1982). *Kinsei Kashihonya no Kenkyū.* Tōkyōtō Shuppan.

Nagatomo, C. (2002). *Edo Jidai no Tosho Ryūtsū.* Shibunkaku Shuppan.

Nakajima, T. (2013). *Iwanami Shigeo: Riberaru Nashonarisuto no Shōzō.* Iwanami Shoten.

Nankatei, M. [pseud.] (1901–1902). "Shosei/fūzoku: Irohaya Kashihon." *Fūzoku Gahō* (227), 31–34, (229), 29–32, (230), 41–43, (233), 30–31, (235), 31–33, (237), 30–31, (238), 34–35, (240), 30–31, (242), 30–33, (243), 33–36.

Nash, E. (2009). *Manga Kamishibai: The Art of Japanese Paper Theater.* New York: Abrams Comicarts.

Neitzel, L. (2016). *The Life We Longed For: Danchi Housing and the Middle Class Dream in Postwar Japan.* Merwinasia.

National Federation of University Co-operative Associations (NFUCA) (2021). "Dai-56-kai gakusei seikatsu jittai-chōsa no gaiyō hōkoku." www.univcoop.or.jp/press/life/report.html

"Nihon-ichi chiisai kamoshirenai honya." (2020). *Chiba Nippō*, November 5. www.chibanippo.co.jp/news/local/737541.

Nihon Zasshi Kyōkai (2012). "Higashi-Nihon Dai-shinsai-go no shuppan-kai no taiō." April 3. www.j-magazine.or.jp/assets/doc/20120403_01 .pdf.

Noppe, N. (2014). "The cultural economy of fanwork in Japan: Dōjinshi exchange as a hybrid economy of open source cultural goods." PhD dissertation. University of Leuven.

Ogawa, T., Okuizumi, K. and Oguro, K. (2016). *Jinbutsu de Tadoru Nihon no Toshokan no Rekishi*. Seikyūsha.

Okamura, K. (1996). *Edo no Zōshokatachi*. Kōdansha.

Okuizumi, K. (2014). *Toshokan-shi no Kakikata/Manabikata: Toshokan no Genzai to Asu wo Kangaeru tameni*. Japan Library Association.

Oldenburg, R. (1989/1997). *The Great Good Place: Cafés, Coffee Shops, Bookstores, Bars, Hair Salons, and Other Hangouts at the Heart of a Community*. Boston, MA: Da Capo Press.

Ōhashi, T. and Yamanaka, T. (2015–2016). *Raito Noberu Furontorain*. 3 vols. Seikyūsha.

Ōsaka Asahi Shinbun. (1923). September 8.

Ōtani, T. (2016). "Kako kara Tsutaya Toshokan wo nagameru." *Jōhō Kanri* 58(10),782–786.

Ōuchi, T. (2009). "Kanda Jinbōchō shoten-machi no seiritsu: Nihonbashi kara Jinbōchō e no ikōki no shomondai." *Mita Shakaigaku* 14, 12–23.

Ōuchi, T., Koyama, N., Fujita, H., and Kumada, T., eds. (2008). *Kanda-Jinbōchō to Hei-on-Wai: Kosho to Machi-zukuri no Hikaku-shakaigaku*. Tōshindō.

Our City Corporation (1982). *Nagoya: Machi no Jiten*. Our City Corporation.

Patessio, M. (2010). "Readers and writers: Japanese women and magazines in the late nineteenth century." In P. F. Kornicki, M. Patessio and G. G.

Rowley, eds., *The Female As Subject: Reading and Writing in Early Modern Japan*. Ann Arbor: Center for Japanese Studies, University of Michigan, pp. 191–213.

Pettegree, A. (2010). "Book town Wittenberg." In *The Book in the Renaissance*. New Haven, CT: Yale University Press, pp. 91–106.

"Popularity of Japanese libraries hitting publishers' bottom line." (2018). *Nippon.com*. December 21. www.nippon.com/en/features/h00356.

"Report of the United States Library Mission to Advise on the Establishment of the National Diet Library of Japan." (1948). October. Department of State (publication 3200).

Robles, P. (2009). "From *toshokan* to *bunko*: Rethinking the public libraries from the view of Japanese grassroots children's libraries." *Asian Studies* 45(1–2), 17–32.

Ross, C. S. (2018). "The company of readers." In C. S. Ross, L.E.F. McKechnie and P. M. Rothbauer, eds., *Reading Still Matters: What the Research Reveals about Reading, Libraries, and Community*. Santa Barbara, CA: Libraries Unlimited, pp. 1–70.

Sanseidō Shoten Hyakunen-shi Kankō Iinkai, ed. (1981). *Sanseidō Shoten Hyakunen-shi*. Sanseidō Shoten.

Satō, S. (2016). "'Tsutaya Toshokan' kara kangaeru kyōiku-kikan toshite no toshokan." *Musa: Hakubutsukan Gakugeiin Katei Nenpō* 30, 21–30.

Satō, T. (2002). *Kingu no Jidai: Kokumin Taishū Zasshi no Kōkyōsei*. Iwanami Shoten.

Sawamura, S. (2020). *Nihon Manga Zenshi: Chōjū Giga kara Kimetsu no Yaiba made*. Heibonsha.

Schencking, J. C. (2013). *The Great Kantō Earthquake and the Chimera of National Reconstruction in Japan*. New York: Columbia University Press.

"Scientific notes and news." (1924). *Journal of the Washington Academy of Sciences* 14 (8) (April 19), 182.

Shiba, R. (1995). *Kaidō wo Yuku, vol. 36: Honjo Fukagawa Sanpo, Kanda Kaiwa*. Asahi Shinbunsha.

Shibano, K. (2008). "Shodana to hiradai: Kindai Nihon ni okeru kōsho kūkan no keisei." *Masu Komyunikēshon Kenkyū* 73, 41–59.

Shimada, M. (2019). *Toshokan/Machi-sodate/Demokurashī: Seto-uchi Shimin Toshokan de Kangaetakoto*. Seikyūsha.

Shimizu, I. (1991). *Manga no Rekishi*. Iwanami Shoten.

Shinchōsha. (2021). "Naoki-shō jūshō-saku *Bitamin F* ga irei no 17-nen-buri hitto de ruikei 85-man-bu koe! Shigematsu Kiyoshi no 'nakeru hon" fea ga zenkoku shoten de kaisaichū." Press release. November 1. https://prtimes.jp/main/html/rd/p/000000380.000047877.html.

Shindō, T. (2017). *Toshokan to Edo Jidai no Hitobito*. Kashiwa Shobō.

Shindō, T. (2019). *Toshokan no Nihonshi*. Bensei Shuppan.

Shiobara, A. (2002). "Shozōsareru shomotsu: Enpon būmu to Kyōyōshugi." *Yokohama Kokudai Kokugo Kenkyū* 20, 1–10.

Shockey, N. (2019). *The Typographic Imagination: Reading and Writing in Japan's Age of Modern Print Media*. New York: Columbia University Press.

Smith, H. D., II (1994). "The history of the book in Edo and Paris." In J. L. McClain, J. M. Merriman, and K. Ugawa, eds., *Edo and Paris: Urban Life and the State in the Early Modern Era*. Ithaca, NY: Cornell University Press, pp. 332–352.

Sōma, A. (1938/1972). *Ichi-shōnin toshite: Shoshin to Taiken*. Iwanami Shoten.

Steinberg, M. (2012). *Anime's Media Mix: Franchising Toys and Characters in Japan*. Minneapolis: University of Minnesota Press.

Sukigara, H. and Taniguchi G. (2002). "Kōkyō toshokan ni okeru dokusho-kōi no kanōsei: Dokusho kūkan ni kansuru Kenkyū." *Nihon Kenchiku Gakkai Taikai Gakujitsu Kōen Kōgaishū* 2002, 125–126.

Suumo Shinchiku Manshon. (2022). Saitama edition. January.

Suzuki, S. (1985). *Nihon no Shuppankai wo Kizuita Hitobito.* Kashiwa Shobō.

Suzuki, S. and Ishii, A., eds. (1967). *Bukku Mobiru to Kashidashi Bunko.* Japan Library Association.

Suzuki, T. (1980). *Edo no Honya.* 2 vols. Chūō Kōronshinsha.

Suzuki, T., Arakawa, A., Koizumi, S. and Takasuna, M. (2016). "CIE libraries supporting the development of psychology during the Allied occupation in Japan (1945–1952)." *Japanese Psychological Research* 58(1) supplement, 19–31.

Taishō Daishinsai Daikasai. (1923). Kōdansha.

Takahashi, M. (1982). "Shuppan ryūtsūkikō no hensen: 1903–1945." *Shuppan Kenkyū* 13, 188–228.

Takano, R. and Hori, M. (2021). "Nihon ni okeru denshi-shoseki-ka no genjō (2020-nenban)." *Nihon Shuppan Gakkai Kaihō* 150(1), 5–6.

Takano, S. (2016). *Kashihon-manga to Sengo no Fūkei.* Ronsōsha.

Takayama, M. (2016). *Rekishi ni Miru Nihon no Toshokan: Chiteki Seika no Juyō to Denshō.* Keisō Shobō.

Takei, K. (2012). "'Sōsharu rīdingu' ga aku dokusho no shinsekai." *Nihon Keizai Shinbun,* December 25. www.nikkei.com/article/DGXNASFK 1901H_Z11C12A200000.

Takeuchi, Y. (2003). *Kyōyōshugi no Botsuraku.* Chūō Kōronshinsha.

Takeuchi, Y. (2018). *Kyōyō-ha Chishikijin no Unmei: Abe Jirō to sono Jidai.* Chikuma Shobō.

Taylor, S. P. (2016). "The uses of a free paper map in the internet age." In K. Wigen, F. Sugimoto and C. Karacas, eds., *Cartographic Japan: A History in Maps.* Chicago, IL: University of Chicago Press, pp. 218–221.

Temple, E. (2012). "The 20 Most Beautiful Bookstores in the World." *Flavorwire.* www.flavorwire.com/254434/the-20-most-beautiful-book stores-in-the-world.

"TikTok de Shojaku wo Shōkai = Bakuhatsuteki Hitto." (2021). *Fujin Kōron*, via *Yahoo News*. October 11. https://news.yahoo.co.jp/articles/80fce6168caa510614118d7d240440b8f798d485.

Tōkyō Asahi Shinbun. (1913). September 12.

Tōkyō Teikoku Daigaku. (1932). *Tōkyō Teikoku Daigaku Gojū-nenshi*. 2 vols. Tōkyō Teikoku Daigaku.

"Tōkyō Kanda-Jinbōchō no Okori" (2020). On blog "Akamarumai no Furusato kara, Ecchū no Sasaraki, nununu!" December 8. https://blog.goo.ne.jp/magohati35/e/307b57fe3f6bc2b79eced3a95530a050.

Toyama, M. (2019). "Kanda-Jinbōchō ni okeru koshoten-machi to kyōiku-kikan no hensen: Fukanzen jōhō ni yoru jikūkan hyōgen shuhō no kentō." *Hōsei Daigaku Daigakuin Deʐain Kōgaku Kenkyūka Kiyō* 8, 1–8.

Toyama, M., Tanaka, S. and Fukui, T. (2018). "Kanda-Jinbōchō koshoten-machi no hassei to hensen." *Keikan/Deʐain Kenkyū Kōenshū* 14, 22–28.

Tokyo Association of Dealers in Old Books (1964). *Kōhon Kanda Koshosekisho-shi*. Tokyo Association of Dealers in Old Books.

Tomozō. (2018). "Wakamono no hon-hanare ga shinkoku: Daigakusei no hansū-ijō ga ichinichi no dokusho jikan ga zero." *Kamiapu* blog. February 28. www.appps.jp/287103.

Travel Note. (2017). "Ikebukuro de ninki no honya matome! Ōki shoten ya tomareru shisetsu mo wadai!" October 19. https://travel-noted.jp/posts/12956.

Tsukuda K., ed. (2012). *Tosho/Toshokanshi* (Gendai Toshokan Jōhōgaku Shiriizu, vol. 11). Jusonbō.

Uchiyama, K. (1960). *Kakōroku*. Iwanami Shoten.

Uchiyama, S. (2005). "Shinsho wo baikai to suru dokusho kūkan: 1950-nendai~60-dai ni okeru shinsho no fukyū ni tsuite." *Jōchi Daigaku Shakaigaku Ronshū* 29, 147–167.

Uemura, T. (1969). *Henbōsuru Shakai: '70-nendai e no Shiten*. Seibundō Shinkōsha.

United Nations (2019). *World Urbanization Prospects: The 2018 Revision.* New York: United Nations.

Wakimura, Y. (1979). *Tōzai Shoshi-machi Kō*. Iwanami Shoten.

Welch, T. F. (1976). *Toshokan: Libraries in Japanese Society*. Chicago, IL: American Library Association.

Welch, T. F. (1997). *Libraries and Librarianship in Japan*. Westport, CT: Greenwood Press.

Wingfield, L. S. (1889). *The Wanderings of a Globe-Trotter in the Far East*. 2 vols. London: Richard Bentley and Son.

Yagi, F. (2007). *Furuhon Unchiku*. Heibonsha.

Yamamoto, M. (2014). *Nihon Kyōikushi: Kyōiku no "Ima" wo Rekishi kara Kangaeru*. Keiō Gijuku Daigaku Shuppankai.

Yamamoto, T. (2019). *Dokushokai Nyūmon: Hito ga Hon de Majiwaru Basho*. Gentōsha.

Yamazaki, H., Li, S. and Yamazaki, E. (2012). *Toshokan to Denshi-shoseki: Haiburiddo Toshokan e*. Kyōiku Shuppan Sentā.

Yamazumi, M. (1987). *Nihon Kyōiku Shōshi: Kin/Gendai*. Iwanami Shoten.

Yorioka, R. and Hoshino, R. (2020). "Bukkufe toiu "ba" ni okeru dokushokai ni tsuite: Chiiki ni okeru dokusho shinkō katsudō no kanten kara." *Gengo Bunka Kenkyū* 28, 165–180.

Yoshino, G. (1964/1988). "Akaban jidai: Henshūsha no omoide." In Iwanami Shoten Henshūbu, ed., *Iwanami Shinsho no 50-nen*. Iwanami Shoten, pp. 127–142.

Acknowledgments

Parts of the research that went into this work were presented at the "Book Cultures, Book Events" conference at the University of Stirling (2012), the "Japan: Premodern, Modern and Contemporary" conference at Dimitrie Cantemir Christian University (2015), and SHARP 2019. I want to thank all the attendees for their comments, in particular my fellow panelists at SHARP 2019, Samantha Rayner and Eben Muse, for their support. Special thanks to all of the individuals and institutions who granted permission for images to be used in this volume: Takano Akihiko and Association Press, Tokyo Association of Dealers in Old Books, Hashiguchi Kōnosuke and Seishindō Shoten, Takasaki City Library, Nippon.com, Tsujimoto Tamako and the staff of TBS, Kadokawa Shoten, Kobayashi Wataru and ANYCOLOR Inc., the NIJISANJI VTubers Fumi and Amemori Sayo, and the artist krs. Thanks are also due to the National Diet and Aoyama Gakuin University Libraries. Finally, I want to thank Samantha Rayner and Eben Muse again for overseeing this book, the two reviewers for their helpful comments, Roger Brown for his comments on Chapter 2, and my partner Rieko Kamei-Dyche for supporting and encouraging me at every step of the way.

For my families on both sides of the world

Cambridge Elements ≡

Publishing and Book Culture

SERIES EDITOR

Samantha Rayner
University College London

Samantha Rayner is Professor of Publishing and Book Cultures at UCL. She is also Director of UCL's Centre for Publishing, co-Director of the Bloomsbury CHAPTER (Communication History, Authorship, Publishing, Textual Editing and Reading) and co-Chair of the Bookselling Research Network.

ASSOCIATE EDITOR

Leah Tether
University of Bristol

Leah Tether is Professor of Medieval Literature and Publishing at the University of Bristol. With an academic background in medieval French and English literature and a professional background in trade publishing, Leah has combined her expertise and developed an international research profile in book and publishing history from manuscript to digital.

About the Series

This series aims to fill the demand for easily accessible, quality texts available for teaching and research in the diverse and dynamic fields of Publishing and Book Culture. Rigorously researched and peer-reviewed Elements will be published under themes, or 'Gatherings'. These Elements should be the first check point for researchers or students working on that area of publishing and book trade history and practice: we hope that, situated so logically at Cambridge University Press, where academic publishing in the UK began, it will develop to create an unrivalled space where these histories and practices can be investigated and preserved.

Cambridge Elements ☰

Publishing and Book Culture

Bookshops and Bookselling

Gathering Editor: Eben Muse

Eben Muse is Senior Lecturer in Digital Media at Bangor University and co-Director of the Stephen Colclough Centre for the History and Culture of the Book. He studies the impact of digital technologies on the cultural and commercial space of bookselling, and he is part-owner of a used bookstore in the United States.

ELEMENTS IN THE GATHERING

A full series listing is available at: www.cambridge.org/EPBC

Printed in the United States
by Baker & Taylor Publisher Services